Safeguarding Adults

Jackie Martin

 Theory into Practice

Series Editor Neil Thompson

RHP

Russell House Publishing

First published in 2007 by:
Russell House Publishing Ltd.
4 St. George's House
Uplyme Road
Lyme Regis
Dorset DT7 3LS
Tel: 01297-443948
Fax: 01297-442722
e-mail: help@russellhouse.co.uk
www.russellhouse.co.uk

British Library Cataloguing-in-publication Data:

A catalogue record for this book is available from the British Library.

ISBN: 978-1-903855-98-0

Typeset by TW Typesetting, Plymouth, Devon
Printed by Biddles, King's Lynn

About Russell House Publishing

RHP is a group of social work, probation, education and youth and community work practitioners and academics working in collaboration with a professional publishing team.

Our aim is to work closely with the field to produce innovative and valuable materials to help managers, trainers, practitioners and students.

We are keen to receive feedback on publications and new ideas for future projects.

For details of our other publications please visit our website or ask us for a catalogue. Contact details are on this page.

Contents

The Theory into Practice Series

This exciting new series fills a significant gap in the market for short, user-friendly texts, written by experts, that succinctly introduce sets of theoretical ideas, relate them clearly to practice issues, and guide the reader to further learning. They particularly address discrimination, oppression, equality and diversity. They can be read either as general overviews of particular areas of theory and practice, or as foundations for further study. The series will be invaluable across the human services, including social work and social care; youth and community work; criminal and community justice work; counselling; advice work; housing; and aspects of health care.

About the Series Editor

Neil Thompson is a Director of Avenue Consulting Ltd (www.avenueconsulting.co.uk), a company offering training and consultancy in relation to social work and human relations issues. He is also a Professor of Social Work and Well-being at Liverpool Hope University. He has over 100 publications to his name, including best-selling textbooks, papers in scholarly journals and training and open learning materials.

Neil is a Fellow of the Chartered Institute of Personnel and Development, the Institute of Training and Occupational Learning and the Royal Society of Arts (elected on the basis of his contribution to organisational learning). He was the founding editor of the *British Journal of Occupational Learning.* He was also responsible for setting up the self-help website, www.humansolutions.org.uk. His personal website is at www.neilthompson.info.

Series Editor's Foreword

About the series

The relationship between theory and practice is one that has puzzled practitioners and theorists alike for some considerable time, and there still remains considerable debate about how the two interconnect. However, what is clear is that it is dangerous to tackle the complex problems encountered in 'people work' without having at least a basic understanding of what makes people tick, of how the social context plays a part in both the problems we address and the solutions we seek. Working with people and their problems is difficult and demanding work. To try to undertake it without being armed with a sound professional knowledge base is a very risky strategy indeed, and potentially a disastrous one.

An approach to practice based mainly on guesswork, untested assumptions, habit and copying others is clearly not one that can be supported. Good practice must be an *informed* practice, with actions based, as far as possible, on reasoning, understanding and evidence. This series is intended to develop just such good practice by providing:

- an introductory overview of a particular area of theory or professional knowledge;
- an exploration of how it relates to practice issues;
- a consideration of how the theory base can help tackle discrimination and oppression; and
- a guide to further learning.

The texts in the series are written by people with extensive knowledge and practical experience in the fields concerned and are intended as an introduction to the wider and more in-depth literature base.

About this book

The 'discovery' of the abuse of children in the 1960s came as a great surprise not only to the general public, but also to very many of the professionals involved in child welfare. We are now in a situation where the abuse of 'vulnerable' adults is beginning to attract media attention and is steadily becoming established as a feature of professional education and training. We are therefore becoming increasingly aware that it is not just children who may need protection from abuse.

This well-written book will therefore prove to be a very useful resource for all staff and managers working with adults in a health and social care context. It provides a careful blend of theory and practice and incorporates helpful guidance on the legal aspects of safeguarding adults from abuse.

A particularly welcome aspect of this book is that it adopts an approach that is critical of essentialist understandings of vulnerability – that is, it rejects the common tendency to see vulnerability as a matter of individual pathology. The author proposes a much more helpful model of vulnerability as being a matter of recognising how powerful social processes can lead to people being victimised. She draws a parallel between the social model of disability (with its emphasis on how social arrangements have the effect of *dis*abling people with a physical impairment) and an understanding of the abuse of vulnerable people as the result of broader social processes of marginalisation, exclusion and stigmatisation. This innovative approach provides a great deal of food for thought and a foundation for empowering forms of practice.

Neil Thompson, Series editor

About the author

Jackie Martin is a senior lecturer at De Montfort University, Leicester, is the programme leader for post-qualifying courses for social workers and teaches on the degree in social work. She has extensive experience of working with adults as well as children and young people in residential settings in both the statutory and voluntary sectors. She has worked for Nottinghamshire Social Services Department as an adult placement scheme co-ordinator, a social worker and team manager in community learning disability teams and as a supervising social worker in a team providing short breaks for disabled children.

Acknowledgements

I wish to thank my family for their support and encouragement in writing this book. Thank you especially Nigel and Kara for proofreading, but thanks also to Tascha and Aiden for their encouragement. Particular thanks go to my friend and former colleague Andy Bigger, for his helpful suggestions and late night reading of the script! I would also like to acknowledge and thank Neil Thompson for his support and direction, which I have found invaluable. Colleagues at De Montfort University and former colleagues and friends from Nottinghamshire County Council have also been very supportive and I thank them for their encouragement.

To the memory of my father, who I will miss always

Introduction

Safeguarding Adults

I make no apology for naming this book after the most recent guidance on the subject, *Safeguarding Adults: A National Framework of Standards for Good Practice and Outcomes in Adult Protection Work.* This was launched in October 2005 by the Association of Directors of Social Services, to provide, as the title says, a framework for good practice and an audit tool kit. The *Framework* does not replace but builds on, an earlier document, *No Secrets: Guidance on Developing and Implementing Multi-Agency Policies and Procedures to Protect Vulnerable Adults from Abuse* (DoH, 2000). Since *No Secrets*, as it will be called throughout this book, talks about 'vulnerable adults', this is now a widely used term among workers. However, this will probably change, as the *Safeguarding Adults* document, as this will be called throughout, adopts the term 'safeguarding adults'.

The purpose of this book

The purpose of this book is twofold. It will look at what you can do if you suspect or know that a person you are working with is subject to abuse and what the options are in terms of interventions. I will also look at the role we can all play in the creation and perpetuation of the experience of being 'vulnerable' for the adults we work with, and explore ways of addressing this.

We live in a world where our attitudes and actions have either a direct or an indirect impact on the lives of others. This is true with our family and friends, but for those of us who work with people, the scope of our influence and power over others is far greater. In some ways I do not think the word 'power' is exact enough to use in this context. Power suggests ability or capacity and a person or a group of people can choose to wield it or not. My argument is that our attitudes and our actions or non-actions which result from these attitudes are apparent and they shape the experience of the adults we work with. It is not a case of us choosing not to use our 'power' as it is demonstrated and felt in every word and action with the people we work with. You may not be aware of how your actions are experienced by others, and part of the purpose of this book is to consider how this happens. One of the most difficult tasks that faces any person is to acknowledge the role they might play in another person's negative experience.

The journey of self-awareness is a long and sometimes painful one, but it is an essential one if we are to work with people in a way that celebrates their uniqueness as individuals rather than add to their negative experience in a society where they are discriminated against.

Language usage is being examined all the time and the ways in which people are actually referred to changes. What is important is that the thinking behind the term is addressed. It is important to consider language: although some people may think that this is merely an example of 'political correctness'. I would like to comment on this accusation now, as it can be a block to people dealing with the issues. The language that people use to refer to others reveals a lot about how they think about them. Thompson (2006) explains:

> Language is part of the social world; indeed, it is one of the bridges between the personal and the social and, as such, it cannot be neutral . . . The language we use either reinforces discrimination through constructing it as 'normal' or contributes, in some small way at least, to undermining the continuance of a discriminatory discourse. (p. 39)

The use of language will be addressed later on when the social model of disability is discussed, but for now I would urge you to keep an open mind and to consider what difference how people are referred to makes to them.

Who is a 'vulnerable adult'?

At the very heart of this book is the importance of what it means to be a 'vulnerable adult'. It therefore seems appropriate to start with a definition. A common sense definition of a 'vulnerable adult' might be a person over eighteen who is 'vulnerable'. This would beg the question as to what the person would be vulnerable to and from whom. It might include nearly everyone at some point in their lives as very few people don't have periods of time where they are vulnerable in some way. 'Vulnerable adults' are actually defined in legislation in terms of their needs for services as well as their vulnerability. Therefore if a person is at risk of abuse or harm, but would not qualify for community care services then they are not referred to as a 'vulnerable adult'. In *No Secrets* (DoH, 2000) a vulnerable adult is someone:

> Who is or may be in need of community care services by reason of mental or other disability, age or illness; and who is or may be unable to take care of him or herself, or unable to protect him or herself against significant harm or exploitation. (DoH, 2000, Section 2.3)

This definition is updated in the *Safeguarding Adults* guidance (ADSS, 2005) to 'every adult "who is or may be eligible for community care services" facing a risk to their independence due to abuse or neglect' (1.14). This shows a development in thinking which will be examined later in this chapter. The principle remains the same, that a person has to be eligible for services, but the emphasis in the second statement is on any risk to independence.

There will be further discussion later in the book about the use of the term 'vulnerable adult', particularly in relation to anti-discriminatory practice and social models. I have already hinted at the fact that you as a worker have a role in shaping the experience of the people you work with. However, for now I will use the term 'vulnerable adults' in the way it is defined above. It is important to note that the definition has two main parts to it and that it includes people who are or may be in need of community care services **and** are unable in some way to care for or protect themselves from harm or exploitation or in the *Safeguarding Adults* definition, at risk of losing their independence. A discussion of what the implication of this definition might be will be included in Part Two of this book. What is obvious is that the definition includes adults with very different needs and who access many different types of community care services. The definition is worded so as to be inclusive rather than provide a list of different categories of service users which may exclude some people by omission. I have not been able to think of any adults that I have worked with that would not come under this definition and I am sure that the definition includes many, if not most, adults with whom care workers, social workers, nurses, other health workers, day centre staff, housing officers, counsellors, people working with adults in supported employment and some college lecturers work every day. As some young people in both 'special' and mainstream schools who would come under the definition stay on at school beyond their eighteenth birthday, it is also relevant to teachers and support staff in schools.

This book is for anyone who works with vulnerable adults. It does examine the responsibilities of different workers if abuse is suspected, but it also discusses the role of attitudes and workplace cultures and practices in the experience of vulnerable adults and how this can be part of the problem rather than the solution.

The difference the way you work makes to people

As a worker working with adults, the way you talk to them, support them, advocate for and with them, listen to them and believe them says more about you than it does them. The way you communicate says something about your communication skills, but it is possible to be the most skilful communicator in the world and still communicate in a way that either directly discriminates against others or patronises and belittles them, giving them the message that they are not your equal or are childlike in some way, even if this is not what you intended. As I have been thinking about what I have seen in practice over the years, I have realised that almost nothing reveals more about how we value the people we work with than the way we speak to and about them. I have worked at many levels: from being a care assistant in a number of Nursing Homes; a residential worker in a special school, as well as in residential units for learning disabled adults; through to being a social worker in a number of different teams; and a Team

Manager of a Community Learning Disability Team. I have been privileged to see many examples of excellent practice at different levels as well as practice which was extremely poor. Over the years my conviction has been strengthened that it is vital to the well-being of adults who are in some way supported by others that those who support them be well versed in themselves as to how they regard people, as this perception shapes the way they work.

Imagine a situation where the experience of older people in a Nursing Home is totally different on different days of the week: some days might be anticipated with relief, whereas others might be anticipated with a sense of dread. The difference to those older people is the staff teams who are on shift on any given day. Some days, the older people know they can look forward to warm, interested conversation and being supported in a gentle and appropriate way. Other days they know a different team will be much rougher in the way they support them, talk to them in an 'off-hand' way and be reluctant to 'allow' the older people the little routines which take time but which is one of the few ways they can put their own individuality on their life in a large institution. The difference between the two types of staff teams will be readily identified by the older people. The first type of team values the older people as individuals, and realises that they have the right to live their lives as individually as they can within the restrictions of their environment, whereas the second type just sees them as so many older people to get ready for bed, to get up or whatever the task is. Both types of teams may be hard-working, efficient and always get the job done and even pride themselves on their work, but with the second team it will be in such a way that produces dread in those who they are 'caring' for. The principle of dignity and worth is implicit in my comments on this scenario. Banks (2006) traces this principle back to Kant:

> This principle is reminiscent of Kant's ultimate principle of 'respect for persons', which entails treating people as ends in themselves and never as a means to an end. It stresses that every human being should be treated in this way, regardless of what they have done. (p.48)

This is an important principle as once you start treating individuals according to how you think they deserve to be treated, you are setting yourselves up in judgment of them in terms of either their actions or capabilities. It is a challenge to us all to recognise that in fact we do, in our minds at least, have opinions and therefore make judgments on those we support. Self-knowledge is vital as only once you recognise that you react to some people more negatively than others, can you begin to address how this shapes your practice. How you support people in a way that respects their worth and promotes their dignity is at the very heart of safeguarding adults.

When I reflect on my experience as a worker and an observer of the work practices of others I have been puzzled by two things. Firstly, why people who are called 'carers' can behave in an uncaring way, and secondly, why people do not challenge other workers when they see or hear of poor practice. The answer to the first question is not necessarily that the workers are 'bad' people; it is more that in some way they regard the people they are caring for as less than themselves. They do not treat them as I'm sure they would like to be treated were the situation to be reversed. This way of thinking may not be at a conscious level and in fact I suspect would be strongly refuted by the worker, but will none the less form part of their belief system and profoundly affect the way they think and how they act.

The answer to the second question is very much what has prompted me to write this book. It is because the person does not feel able or compelled to challenge the practice of others who may be far more experienced, perhaps older and more confident. As my confidence grew as a carer and then as a qualified social worker and manager, I gained the necessary knowledge and confidence in my own judgment to be able to challenge the practice of others as well as reflect on my own, although I will not pretend that I ever found it easy. However, I remember only too well the occasions early on in my career when I did not speak up for those who were unable to do so for themselves. My own practice may have been good, but that was not really good enough. It is not an option to take a passive position. If I kept quiet rather than spoke up on behalf of people by challenging practice, then I was just as much a part of the problem as those who practiced poorly. It is not always possible to go back and challenge situations that should have been challenged in the past, although if it relates to suspicions of abuse this should be discussed with the relevant professionals, even if it was not reported at the time. What is important is that you behave in ways which show respect and address issues of unfair or dehumanising treatment or abuse either with the service user or on their behalf. Everything you do as well as don't do is the result of two things: firstly, where you are in your own understanding of what it is you are trying to achieve; and secondly, your attitude towards the people you are working with.

What your practice says about you

What you believe and the way you think and act says more about who you are than it does about the people you support or work alongside. It does not matter whether you are a qualified worker or not, the issues are exactly the same. This sounds obvious and maybe simple, but it takes a lifetime of continued thought to address the issue of who you are and how this impacts on others. It is part of the purpose of this book to examine what is meant by the term 'vulnerable adult', but equally it examines the role that you have not only in terms of possibly being alert to, or investigating abuse, but in addressing environments, practices, attitudes and cultures which lead to the oppression and sometimes the abuse of adults.

All who work with adults have a role in safeguarding them. What your role is depends on your job, but whatever your job is, you have an important part to play in safeguarding the adults you work with.

How this book is structured

The book aims to provide an introduction to the field of safeguarding adults and will examine the theoretical base as well as practice issues. It is divided into four parts.

Part One explores the theoretical base for safeguarding adults. In Chapter 1 the definition of and types of abuse are examined as well as the concept of human rights and principles in relation to mental capacity. Chapter 2 explores a parallel between the concept of a 'vulnerable adult' and the analysis of the concept of disability as expressed in the social model of disability. It examines issues raised by two case studies and explores principles which should govern practice as well as the concept of 'empowerment'.

Part Two is concerned with links between theory and practice. It examines the legal framework and responsibilities of all who work with adults. Chapter 3 discusses the definition of a 'vulnerable adult'. The chapter goes on to look at government strategies in relation to safeguarding adults and the responsibilities that arise from them for all who work with adults. What actually happens when a concern is raised and then reported is explored. Different options are discussed in terms of interventions when abuse is suspected. Chapter 4 examines issues in relation to family carers and looks at their role with those they care for as well as how they can be seen in the context of structural oppression. The complexities of working with carers are identified and practice issues explored through case study and discussion. Carers' own needs are acknowledged as well as risk factors which could lead to the person they are caring for being abused or supported inappropriately. Chapter 5 explores the concept of 'service user involvement'. It discusses involvement in the planning and reviewing of services as well as in adult protection interventions. It links service user involvement with the realisation of citizen rights. The role that advocacy services can play in safeguarding adults is also explored in this chapter.

Part Three is concerned with ways in which theory addresses discrimination and oppression. It uses Thompson's PCS analysis to identify ways in which discrimination is perpetuated and emphasises the role of family and workplace culture in the creation and continuation of either good or poor ways of working with adults. The role that our values play in the way we support individuals is examined and this includes a discussion of religious beliefs.

Part Four offers suggestions for further reading as well as useful websites.

Part One: The Theory Base

Chapter 1
Definitions, Rights and Issues of Capacity

This part of the book is concerned with the theoretical basis for safeguarding adults. Safeguarding adults is not just about adult protection, although this is an important element of it. It is also about supporting adults through service provision (which includes assessments) in a way which respects them and their rights as citizens. However, I will start with an examination of what constitutes abuse as defined in *No Secrets* (DoH, 2000) and then move on to what the Human Rights Act 1998 says about people's rights in relation to service provision from statutory agencies. Lastly in this chapter, I will examine the concept of mental capacity, as an understanding of this is vital if people are to be afforded their rights rather than denied them by false assumptions being made about them.

How you view abuse is partly the result of your own upbringing, education, experience and culture. It is therefore important that you constantly measure the outcomes of the services you provide for adults against these definitions. If anything we do either individually or collectively results in an adult receiving an abusive service, then practices need to be re-examined and changed.

What is abuse?

Abuse will be referred to extensively in this book and it might seem obvious what it is. However, I have heard many discussions between workers who were trying to decide whether a particular situation was actually abusive or not, so perhaps it is not such a matter of common sense as would first appear. *No Secrets* acknowledges that the term 'abuse' can be open to interpretation but gives a definition as a starting point:

> Abuse is a violation of an individual's human and civil rights by any other person or persons. (2.5)

The document then goes on to stress that abuse may consist of single or repeated acts. It can be physical, verbal or psychological, an act of neglect or an omission to act. It can be when a 'vulnerable person' is persuaded to enter into an agreement the nature of which they do not understand, such as of a financial or sexual nature and to which they have not consented or cannot consent. The document goes on to state that abuse can occur in any relationship and 'may result in significant harm to, or exploitation of, the person subjected to it' (2.6). The fact that some abuse can result in 'significant harm' is acknowledged, the corollary of which is that not all abuse does lead to 'significant harm'. This is an interesting point and one worthy of some discussion. The meaning of 'significant' here has a number of issues attached to it. The question, 'significant for whom?' is an obvious one and the response would also seem obvious in that it would be the person concerned. However, what if the person doesn't deem a situation to be significant when all others do, or what if a person is unable to say (for whatever reason) whether or not they deem a situation to be significant? Who then decides if the situation leads to 'significant harm'? It would seem from *No Secrets* that a situation can be abusive, but not lead to 'significant harm'. Here is a really interesting and thought-provoking point. *Safeguarding Adults* (ADSS, 2005) views abuse as an experience which stops adults enjoying their independence and rights as citizens. Is not every act, system, process or institution that stops an adult realising their rights, causing them 'significant harm'? Is 'harm' accepted as a phenomenon which a person is aware of and experiences as such, or can it be viewed as the more insidious experience of being in environments and with people who do not treat adults as equals? When the document refers to 'harm', it is referring to the first of these possibilities, but in the context of providing services, it is important to be mindful of the second. I would want to maintain that the experience of being devalued as a person is harmful and that 'harm' is extremely significant as it pervades the self-worth of individuals. If a person is treated without respect consistently, then it is very difficult for them to gain or maintain a sense of self-worth.

As far as *No Secrets* is concerned, however, abuse *can* lead to significant harm, but does not necessarily do so. The document outlines different forms of abuse and gives examples of each and lists:

Physical abuse.
Sexual abuse.
Psychological abuse.
Financial or material abuse.
Neglect and acts of omission.
Discriminatory abuse (2.7).

I shall discuss each of these categories as defined in *No Secrets* and provide some comments to help you think through the implications of what the document says for your own practice and for practice which you might observe.

Physical abuse

Under the category of physical abuse, together with the more obvious examples such as hitting, slapping, pushing and kicking, are listed 'misuse of medication, restraint, or inappropriate sanctions'. These in turn are open to interpretation and involve complex decisions. It clearly seems abusive to over-medicate someone so that they are in a semi-stupor. However, medication is often used to calm someone down who otherwise gets very anxious and can be a part of a legitimate medical intervention. How far is the medication used for the benefit of the person themselves and how far is it used for the 'benefit' of the people living with them or supporting them? Is it abusive if a person is medicated to stop them being so anxious and thereby enabling the person 'caring' for them to continue with this task when they might not be able to cope with the level of anxiety expressed? These are all judgments which need to be balanced and thought through carefully. This is not an area where everything is clear-cut. Some acts are very clearly abusive, but others are not so obvious. Each circumstance will have to be examined in its context. A residential home where people are *routinely* over-medicated so that they are 'calm' is an example of an abusive regime. Some people may need to be on high dosages of medication but others may not. It is the responsibility of health professionals not to oversubscribe, but they often rely on the opinions of people supporting the individual to make their judgments about dosages.

'Restraint', as it is called in *No Secrets*, or physical intervention, is not seen as abusive, but again its 'misuse' is. There are circumstances where people have to have physical interventions for their own or others' safety. However, where there is a culture of physical intervention as an almost automatic response to behaviour that challenges, then this is abusive. Each setting where physical restraint is used should have clear guidelines on its use. It should also provide training for staff in its use and crucially, the training should facilitate an awareness of when it is inappropriate and therefore abusive. Section 6 of the Mental Capacity Act 2005 defines restraint as 'the use or threat of force where an incapacitated person resists, and any restriction of liberty or movement whether or not the person resists'. It states that it is only permitted when the person using it reasonably believes it is necessary to prevent harm and the physical intervention used has to be proportionate 'to the likelihood and seriousness of the harm'.

'Inappropriate sanctions' is a highly value laden concept. When is a sanction inappropriate? Is it the sanction itself or the use in an inappropriate way that makes it abusive? Again there are instances where it is clear that the use of some sanctions is abusive, for example if they hurt or degrade a person. As it is listed under 'physical abuse', this would suggest sanctions that actually harm the individual physically are being referred to. It is certainly important to think through the use of any form of sanction or 'reward'. There is a fine distinction between withholding a reward and imposing a sanction. There might be circumstances where a reward system is totally appropriate but it is also a system which is open to misuse and can become abusive. The important thing here is to think through why things are done and what the effect is on the person. Does the system allow them to enjoy their rights and experience independence or does it demean and dishearten them thus adding to their negative experience?

Sexual abuse

Sexual abuse includes rape and sexual assault or sexual acts to which the adult did not or could not consent. I will examine the law in relation to consent in Part Two and make the point that the law has changed and it is now a criminal offence to commit a sexual act with a person who is unable to consent to it. One difficult area in this regard is when sexual acts take place between two people who are deemed as unable to consent or at least did not fully understand what they were consenting to. There is a real debate here in relation to the rights of individuals to have a relationship if they choose to and their right to be protected against being pressured into acts which they do not understand or anticipate. To support people in their lives so that they can choose to have relationships if they want them is a very skilled and important area of work. Issues such as these often raise very strong feelings amongst family members as well as professional workers. It is important that the focus is on supporting people to make informed decisions.

Psychological abuse

Psychological abuse includes 'emotional abuse, threats of harm or abandon-ment, deprivation of contact, humiliation, blaming, controlling, intimidation, coercion, harassment, verbal abuse, isolation or withdrawal from services or supportive networks'. Clearly this covers a huge range of different acts towards individuals. Some of the acts seem on the surface to be fairly straightforward, such as 'isolation or withdrawal from services or supportive networks'. However, when this is examined a little more closely, this could include practices such as 'allowing' a person space and time to 'calm down'. Again, this may be totally appropriate and may meet a psychological need of the adult. It could, on the other hand, be an abusive practice and be more to punish, or to meet the needs of the people supporting the individual. The importance of re-examining such practice issues cannot be overstated, as the implications for the lives of the adults in such situations are far-reaching. Emotional abuse can be difficult to quantify, but if I begin with the premise that it is treatment or practices which result in emotional harm then it provides a starting point from which to examine practice. Given the context of the *Safeguarding Adults* philosophy that abuse prevents adults from gaining or maintaining independence, the question to apply to practices could be whether they impair an individual's ability to be independent. By independence it does not mean that a person is able to be totally independent without any support or they would not qualify for community care services in the first place. What is referred to is the fact that a person is assessed under the FACS guidance (*Fair Access To Care Services*, DoH, 2002) in terms of risks to their independence. Any abuse would present as a risk to independence and is linked in the guidance to 'autonomy and freedom to make choices, health and safety including freedom from harm, abuse and neglect, housing and community safety'. A question to ask of practices is whether they enhance or impair an individual's ability to make choices and be autonomous. If the practice itself, rather than any other factor, is impairing the person's ability then it would suggest that the practice itself is abusive. It may not always be a straight forward question, but it is none the less an important one to ask.

Financial abuse

Financial or material abuse is said in No Secrets to include 'theft, fraud, exploitation, pressure in connection with wills, property or inheritance or financial transactions, or the misuse or misappropriation of property, possessions or benefits'. My experience as a social worker and manager tells me that this is the most difficult form of abuse to detect and prove. The misappropriation of benefits can be a very difficult issue to address with some families who see the benefits as belonging to the family rather than the individual. The situation can be made more complex if the adult concerned does not want the issue addressed as this could upset relationships within their family. There are huge issues in terms of older people especially, but not only them, in relation to wills for instance. It can be very difficult for outside workers to be clear about what is really happening inside a family unit when the older person may be physically dependent on those who they live with.

Neglect

Neglect and acts of omission include 'ignoring medical or physical care needs, failure to provide access to appropriate health, social care or educational services, the withholding of the necessities of life, such as medication, adequate nutrition and heating'. As will be detailed in Part Two, under the Mental Capacity Act 2005 it is now an offence to neglect a person who lacks capacity.

Discriminatory abuse

Discriminatory abuse includes abuse that is 'racist, sexist, that based on a person's disability, and other forms of harassment, slurs or similar treatment' (No Secrets 2.7). I will be examining issues in relation to discriminatory abuse in Part Three.

Human Rights

Key to any understanding of abuse is an appreciation of human rights, as the No Secrets definition cited at the beginning of this chapter would indicate. The Human Rights Act 1998 imposes limits on those in authority in how they can act towards individuals. The European Convention on Human Rights is included within the 1998 Act. Article 2 from the Convention establishes a 'right to life'. This is a basic right and means that failure to protect an adult against actions or omissions which cause their death is a breach of this right and local authorities could be sued if this happens. New legislation as cited in Part Two makes it an offence to cause the death of an adult through neglect. It might sound like very straight forward decisions can be reached in order to prevent such terrible events, but often it means that workers have to pursue investigations without the type of legal provision afforded to child care workers under the Children Act 1989. There is not the power to remove an adult from their home for assessment purposes apart from under the Mental Health Act 1983 and even if there was, that in itself would probably be in contravention of a person's rights. This means that this is a complex area of work and requires great skill in correctly assessing situations and gathering information from multiple sources.

Article 3 of the Convention is the right not to be subjected to 'inhuman or degrading treatment'. This clearly fits within the category of 'psychological abuse' as detailed in *No Secrets*. The implication of this for service delivery is that adults must not be subjected to inhuman or degrading treatment by workers. It also has implications for preventative measures in that an adult should not be subjected to such treatment in any setting and therefore should be protected from such treatment. What actually constitutes 'inhuman or degrading treatment' is a matter of debate. Any practice or acts towards a person which devalue them as people could come under this category. However, the European Court of Human Rights has stated that such treatment must reach a minimum level of severity which involves actual bodily injury or intense physical or mental suffering. Degrading treatment could occur if it 'humiliates or debases an individual showing a lack of respect for, or diminishing, his or her dignity or arouses feelings of fear, anguish or inferiority capable of breaking an individual's moral and physical resistance' (*Pretty v United Kingdom*, cited in Mandelstam, p. 481).

Article 5 of the Convention provides a 'right to liberty and security'. This means that people cannot be detained unless a lawful procedure is followed. The Bournewood case is an example of this, where a person was detained (*HL v United Kingdom*) without any legal protection so the detention was found to be in contravention of Article 5. This set an important precedent as following this case, when an adult is detained, but not under the Mental Health Act 1983, the adult has to have built in to their care plan safeguards for them such as the right to appeal, to have their case reviewed and an independent person taking part in decisions. This presents a real issue for people who provide a service for adults who may need an environment which keeps them safe if, for example, they are at risk from wandering into the street and getting lost or causing a road traffic accident. This is an area where a great deal of thought needs to go into how people are supported in a way which maximises their independence but also ensures their safety.

Article 8 provides a right 'to respect for family life and private life'. This means that any interference in people's lives must be absolutely necessary and lawful. This seems to be clearer in child protection issues as this involves the use of compulsory powers under the Children Act 1989. In work with adults, where abuse is suspected and workers intervene they might be acting in a necessary way, but the intervention must also be lawful. This means that families and individuals should be worked with in a way which respects their lives but at the same time addresses issues of possible abuse. I will look at some possible legal interventions in cases of adult abuse in Part Two, but this Article must always be borne in mind with such interventions and inform any decisions to intervene in people's lives.

It is your responsibility to understand the implications of people's rights for how you practice. If it is part of your role to make decisions in relation to interventions, you must weigh up any possible interventions against the rights of individuals and the effect it will have on their independence.

Mental Capacity

One question not yet addressed is that of capacity. If a person does not have capacity, how does this affect the way they are supported?

The Mental Capacity Act 2005 is underpinned by five key principles which are stated in section 1:

- A presumption of capacity – every adult has the right to make his or her own decisions and must be assumed to have capacity to do so unless it is proved otherwise;
- The right of individuals to be supported to make their own decisions – people must be given all appropriate help before anyone concludes that they cannot make their own decisions;
- That individuals must retain the right to make what might be seen as eccentric or unwise decisions;
- Best interests – anything done for or on behalf of people without capacity must be in their best interests; and
- Least restrictive intervention – anything done for or on behalf of people without capacity should be the least restrictive of their basic rights and freedoms.

The Mental Capacity Act 2005 does not view 'capacity' or a lack of capacity as an all encompassing statement about a person. Rather, it sees 'capacity' as being in relation to specific decisions and it sets out a single test to determine whether a person has capacity for a specific decision at a specific time. Under the Act, people cannot be labelled as being incapable as a result of a diagnosis or condition. This means that issues of capacity will have to be determined at relevant points in a person's life. This is very positive as it will hopefully mean that assumptions are not made about people and that their capacity will be assumed in relation to decisions unless proved otherwise. This is relevant for adult protection issues where action may be taken on behalf of an individual if they do not have capacity such as in an application for declaratory relief, a possible legal intervention which will be examined in Part Two.

The five principles of the Act state how people should be supported. They put people's rights as central and even support the right to make 'eccentric or unwise decisions'. This is an area which I am sure will provoke much discussion as to the differences between 'unwise' and 'unsafe' decisions. It is often very difficult for workers to see people make decisions which they think are the 'wrong' decisions and not to intervene. It is of course important to talk to people about their decisions and assist them in seeing the implications of their decisions, but it is still seen as a right to make mistakes. While this can be difficult for workers, for example if someone chooses to stay with an abusive partner, it is essential that this freedom is preserved. If people do not have the right to make 'mistakes', if indeed that is what they are, then we will end up in a society where people's lives are dictated to them. This freedom is part of being independent and therefore part of our role in safeguarding adults. If a person is assessed as not having capacity, then the last principle says that any intervention must be the least restrictive of people's basic rights and freedoms. I would suggest that this is a sound principle in relation to any intervention and obviously requires careful consideration to decide an appropriate intervention which will safeguard the adult in a way which is the least restrictive to their rights.

Chapter 2
'Vulnerability'

In this chapter I want to explore the concept of 'vulnerability'. It is important to understand the ideas behind this concept, as *Safeguarding Adults* is concerned not only with issues of adult abuse, but, as already stated, with the provision of environments and services which support adults in their rights as individuals. If 'vulnerability' is viewed as being caused by environments and practices, then it strengthens the case for examining these environments and practices. If 'vulnerability' is seen as being innate to certain individuals then the responsibility of workers seems to be more to protect. It is important that you don't confuse vulnerability with needs. I am not denying that people have needs, but I *am* saying that it is something outside of the individual that creates vulnerability. Part of safeguarding adults is to address issues which are more about practice than about the needs of individuals, although the two are of course linked, as practice should never be isolated from a consideration of the needs of the adults you work with.

Parallel with the social model of disability

As I have noted, *Safeguarding Adults* accepts the problems associated with the term 'vulnerable adults' and instead talks of the 'increased vulnerability' of some adults to abuse for the reasons listed in Chapter 1. This still does not get away from the difficulties originally associated with the term, since although it seems to assume that all adults are vulnerable and some are more vulnerable than others, it still leaves the deficit with the adult rather than with their environment. This is not just a matter of words, an argument over semantics. I would like to draw a parallel argument to that used to express the idea of 'disabling environments' rather than disabled people. The social model of disability states that some people do have mental or physical impairments, but it is not these that limit and restrict their inclusion in society. It is not the fact that a person uses a wheelchair to mobilise that means they cannot access some buildings. It is the fact that society constructs buildings which are known to be non-accessible to some members of that society. A person with a learning disability may take a lot longer to learn some skills than other people, but it may not be this fact that disables them. What disables them may be that family and carers assume they will never learn and so always do certain tasks for them. Attitudes are disabling in that they take away the rights of some people to live in ways that others are able to enjoy. Some people may need support in terms of equipment or maybe someone actually supporting them in a task, but this does not mean they are incapable of performing these tasks. Oliver (1996) explains the difference between impairment and disability:

> In our view, it is society which disables physically impaired people. Disability is something imposed on top of our impairments by the way we are unnecessarily isolated and excluded from full participation in society. Disabled people are therefore an oppressed group in society. To understand this it is necessary to grasp the distinction between the physical impairment and the social situation, called 'disability', of people with such impairment. Thus we define impairment as lacking part of or all of a limb, or having a defective limb, organ or restriction of activity caused by a contemporary social organisation which takes no or little account of people who have physical impairments and thus excludes them from participation in the mainstream of social activities. Physical disability is therefore a particular form of oppression. (p. 22)

In the same way, it is societal processes which create vulnerability. People who are called 'vulnerable adults' may be in need of community services to enjoy independence, but this is not what makes them vulnerable. What makes them vulnerable is the way they are treated by society generally and more specifically by those who support them. Vulnerability is therefore also a particular form of oppression.

Discrimination

Discrimination against disabled people is endemic in our society and it is hard to think outside of the mental framework which it gives each of us. It is difficult to see that it is what happens in society which is at fault for excluding and marginalising disabled people. Care has to be taken here, however, not to apportion blame to a society and therefore create a sense of hopelessness in people who feel that they cannot possibly work against the whole of the society. It is the societal processes which disable people. It is the way policies are written and implemented, the manner in which transport is organised, people are recruited or buildings are designed which disables people. Societal processes are particularly disabling when they are seen as running in parallel with a charity model where disabled people are seen as worthy recipients of our charity. This charity model has the effect of stopping us looking at what is actually disabling people, as it makes us feel better about ourselves if we can do something to help these 'unfortunate' people. These two attitudes have the effect of reinforcing each other, making us think that disabled people need 'special' treatment in some way. They don't need 'special' treatment, but do need (as we all do) society to *include* them, rather than build buildings and transport systems that are not accessible, communicate in ways that are unintelligible to them and treat them as less than ourselves, which is what we mean by 'special'.

Just as societal processes are the vehicle by which people are oppressed because society is as it is, rather than the recipients of its discrimination are as they are; so it is in and through society that adults are made vulnerable. They are not vulnerable because they are learning disabled or have a sensory impairment or have dementia, they are vulnerable because of how they will be treated in society. They are 'vulnerable' because individuals and institutions treat them as less than equals, or in other words, treat them in an abusive way. The deficit is not with the adult, but with the values and practice of those that patronise or abuse.

There are, of course, ways in which individuals are at risk of being injured as a result of their own cognitive impairment, and this is not a denial of that. An example of this would be that someone with a lack of awareness of road safety could be injured if they crossed a road by themselves, without the necessary support required to ensure they crossed safely. You may think this person is 'vulnerable' as they could be injured without support. However, there are two points to be made here.

Firstly, an individual in that situation would need support to ensure their safety and that of others who could also be injured in a potential road traffic accident. This is no different in principle to a physically disabled person who might need a wheelchair to enable them to be independent in terms of their mobility. Any of us are 'vulnerable' in that sense, if we are put in a situation for which we are not equipped or prepared. I can no longer read the small print on road maps without my glasses so I have to ensure I remember to take them with me when driving in case I get lost. FACS guidance (DoH, 2002) emphasises that risks to independence should be identified and that will obviously vary from person to person. Under FACS guidance, a person is understood as being at risk of not realising independence and one of the reasons for this might be due to abuse. The guidance does not categorise people as being 'vulnerable'.

Secondly, when we are considering people in abusive situations, it is important that the situation or people causing the situation are seen as 'victimising' rather than something innate in the person causing the vulnerability. There are sometimes complex situations where the person caring for or supporting someone is experiencing a great deal of stress and these issues will be considered in the chapter on family carers. However, to regard the person as 'vulnerable' places the 'problem' with them rather than with a situation in or with a society which has allowed such a situation to develop in which a carer is left to cope with demands beyond their personal resources.

I would like you to consider two case studies at this point which I hope will highlight some of the issues already discussed and help you develop them in your thinking. Although these are fictitious case studies, they are based on elements from actual cases.

Case study 1

Susan is a white middle aged woman with a moderate learning disability. When she was younger, she lived in a long stay hospital which was closed and she then moved into a small residential home. Susan is known by the staff for displaying 'challenging behaviour', by which they mean that she can get very upset and will stamp her feet, shout and sometimes throw whatever is in her hand at the time. Some of the staff group are a little frightened of Susan as they find her unpredictable and are alarmed when she shouts. One day a member of staff notices that Susan has what looks like fingertip bruising on her wrist and upper arm. The member of staff decides not to report her observation as she thinks that someone might have grabbed her, but she can understand this as Susan is so 'difficult'.

Case study 2

Stan is a white older man who has dementia. He lives in a large residential home. There are a large number of older people to support in the home and so staff sometimes take 'shortcuts' in how they support people. One such shortcut is that as Stan wanders around it is sometimes easier to support him in some personal care tasks while he is in communal areas. An example of this is that staff will often shave him while he is sitting with other residents in the lounge. Staff are careful not to do this when his family might be visiting as they know this will upset them as their perception is that Stan used to be a very proud and private man and wouldn't have liked the thought of this happening to him. Staff however, have discussed this informally between themselves and have come to the conclusion that Stan doesn't mind now and it is easier for him, so they do not see what the problem is.

Discussion

Both of these cases concern individuals who classify as a 'vulnerable adult' under *No Secrets*. In the first case study Susan has been bruised by an unknown person. The member of staff who notices the bruising has made a value judgment that Susan is 'difficult' and therefore in some way deserving of the bruises. This judgment is directly influenced by her view of Susan. The member of staff is a little afraid of Susan and this influences her thinking in a number of ways. Firstly, she thinks that Susan may have deserved whatever happened to her. Secondly, Susan lives a life which is full of incidents, and so one more incident would not upset Susan in the way that the member of staff would be upset if someone grabbed her and bruised her arm. Thirdly, Susan probably won't be able to tell her what had happened, even if she were to ask her, as she gets people's names confused. These attitudes may or may not be expressed openly, but nonetheless influence what the member of staff does. The member of staff would not express it as such, but she views Susan as less of a person than herself. She does not think Susan is capable of being truly upset at such an incident so it does not matter as much as if it were another member of staff who was assaulted. This is an example of an attitude which I have encountered numerous times expressed by staff members either directly or indirectly. While attitudes such as this prevail, adults will not be safeguarded, but will be victimised and signs of abuse ignored. I am not minimising the difficulties of supporting a person who might display behaviour which can challenge others. However, in such an environment staff should be supported in understanding the causes of behaviour and although this is always important, it seems especially so when someone has been in a large long stay institution. Any number of external 'triggers' might make a person worried or anxious as they remind them of previous experiences and so cause them to display and communicate the resulting emotions.

Under the *Safeguarding Adults* philosophy, it is the duty of workers who work with Susan to ensure that the environment is non-abusive. In the case study, there are at least three failures to do this. Firstly, Susan has been assaulted by someone; it might be another resident, a member of staff, a visitor, someone who she meets in the day. Whoever it is, the incident has happened and Susan has been assaulted. Secondly, the member of staff has a clear duty to report her observation to the appropriate person and does not do so. Thirdly, there is the general attitude of the member of staff. It seems an impossibility to me for a member of staff to support a person appropriately when they view them in the way described. This is partly at least a training and possibly a recruitment issue. Supporting a person with complex needs and behaviour patterns which are outside the experience of many people requires a positive attitude towards them and skill in how to support them. Understanding behaviour is essential if an environment is to be provided which safeguards adults rather than misunderstands and further discriminates against them.

In the second case study, Stan is supported with his personal care needs in a way which does not respect his dignity. Staff may have thought it through and decided that as Stan doesn't seem to mind then it is acceptable to shave him in the lounge. The practice is demeaning of him as a person and a denial of how he would have wanted to be supported if he were asked prior to his dementia. Such practice does not stem from an environment which safeguards adults, but rather one which looks for easier ways of working for the staff members and which is not afraid to ignore the views of family members, not to mention the right everyone has to dignity and privacy.

Again, I am not underestimating the difficult issues there are in supporting someone with dementia and the value judgments which have to be made in complex situations. Nor am I minimising the skill and often patience required to support someone while they are confused, disorientated and perhaps agitated. I am maintaining that in this instance the environment is the cause of the lack of respect for Stan. He has dementia, but that does not cause the staff to treat him in this disrespectful way. The cause of the disrespect again comes down to the attitude of staff. They view Stan as less than he was. When he was more lucid and able to express an opinion, they almost certainly would not have treated him in this way. Now that he is confused and doesn't object, they feel at liberty to treat him differently.

Principles which govern practice

The role of different professionals may vary depending on the context and the setting. It could be a health, educational, day care, therapeutic, residential or any other setting. The principles which need to be applied to govern the way in which you work are the same:

1. Value the person as an individual.
2. Respect the rights of individuals.
3. Treat the individual with dignity.
4. Ensure that the focus of your work keeps the individuals you are working with at the centre.

The term 'empowerment' is often used by people supporting adults in a very general way and tends to have the connotation of facilitating someone to do something they want to do. The use of the word in this way has had the effect of somewhat devaluing it as a concept and robbing it of its more radical significance. Another way of understanding the concept is as expressed by Thompson (1998):

> Central to the notion of empowerment, as used in the context of emancipatory theory and practice, is the potential for social amelioration, a belief in the possibility and value of people working towards a more just and equal society. (p. 75)

Understood in this context, empowerment is not just about individual actions, but it is about social justice. This concept is very relevant to our understanding of how we as people supporting adults or providing them with services, should act. Individual actions are indeed important and as already intimated can have a great influence on the lives of adults we support. It is not enough for us as individual workers to think through our own role in empowering others, although this is important. How adults are disempowered by society and the services in which they find themselves, also needs careful consideration. This will be addressed in Part Three, but for now it is important to stress that our role as individual workers is only part of the picture.

Points to ponder

I would suggest the following questions are considered either individually or perhaps as discussion starters for team meetings or training days. Some of the questions might be more appropriate for individual reflection first, rather than just giving simplistic answers which people think might be the 'right' response.

➤ How do I view the people I/we support?

➤ Are the people I/we support of equal value to me/us?

➤ Given that all adults should be equal in terms of their rights, are there any practices which I/we have which do not value the adults I/we support as having equal rights?

➤ Think about the 'way things are' in your work in terms of processes and practices. Do these keep the people you are supporting at the centre or do they make them peripheral?

Part Two: Implications for Practice

Chapter 3
Legal and Policy Context

This chapter will trace recent developments in the guidance given in relation to vulnerable adults, starting with *No Secrets* (DoH, 2000) and then with the philosophy and practice guidance as expressed in *Safeguarding Adults* (ADSS, 2005). *No Secrets* was launched on 20 March 2000 by the Department of Health as policy guidance under section 7 of the Local Authority Social Services Act 1970, which gives it the status of statutory guidance. In other words, although it has not quite the same status as statute, it is much stronger than the word 'guidance' would imply and has to be followed unless a really good argument for not doing so can be put forward. It is an extremely important document as it set out for the first time expectations in relation to the protection of vulnerable adults. It requires Local Authorities to have in place the necessary safeguards to recognise and respond to abuse and to work with other agencies to draw up policies and procedures for the protection of adults.

Definition of 'vulnerable adult'

The definition of a vulnerable adult as defined in the *No Secrets* guidance has already been cited (see page 2). In fact, the definition has become progressively more inclusive since the 1991 definition of the Association of Directors of Social Services (ADSS) which listed a number of different client groups which made up the more inclusive category of being a 'vulnerable adult':

- the elderly and very frail;
- those who suffer from mental illness including dementia;
- those who have a sensory or physical disability;
- those who have a learning disability, and
- those who suffer from severe physical illness. (ADSS, 1991)

The present definition (ADSS, 2005) is to be welcomed as any list of service user groups always excludes some people even if the list is meant to be a 'catch all'. The 1991 list above does not mention people with Aspergers syndrome for example, although some people with that diagnosis may need community care services and may be unable to protect themselves against exploitation. The use of the term 'the elderly' in the 1991 document is unfortunate as it groups all older people together and gives them a name which has negative associations. It would be more valuing of older people to refer to them as 'older people' or 'elders'. The role of language in being a vehicle for expressing as well as perpetuating discrimination has already been mentioned and will be further discussed in Part Three.

The fact that the *No Secrets* definition (DoH, 2000) says the term 'vulnerable adult' refers to people in receipt of, or who may be in need of, community care services puts its context as being the National Health Service and Community Care Act 1990 (NHSCCA). It is under this Act that adults are assessed as being in need of community services. In fact, statutory agencies are not legally able to offer services or even commission services without first having carried out a full assessment of need, except in emergency situations. The implication of this is that if a referral regarding possible abuse is made to a local authority in relation to a person they have not previously assessed, they have to make a decision as to whether to include that individual in the adult protection procedures. The person may well be someone who they assess as being in need of community care services, but at the point of referral this is not always clear. To think through why it is important to determine whether or not someone would be assessed as being in need of services takes us right to the heart of the reason for special provision being made for some rather than all adults. The context of policies for protecting vulnerable adults is an assumption that redress is obtained through the legal system. It has been the experience of some groups of individuals that they have not been able to access legal redress as readily as others. Examples of this have been particularly with adults who are learning disabled or have mental health needs as well as others who may have difficulty in accurately recalling events or for whom the court process is too much of an ordeal. Adult protection procedures have been developed to provide a means for these adults to address, or have addressed on their behalf, situations in which they have been wronged in some way.

The legislation discussed in this book is relevant for both England and Wales as they have primary community care law in common (Mandelstam, 2005, p. 403). The National Assembly for Wales has published its own equivalent to *No Secrets* (NAFW, 2000). Scotland has different community care legislation and guidance and although this book does not discuss them, the principles outlined in it are universally applicable.

Why support may be needed to access the legal system

The legal system is a system where adults can seek legal redress for wrongs against them such as being assaulted or having something stolen from them. There are some groups of people that are much more unlikely to be successful in court proceedings than others. There are a number of reasons for this:

1. Many instances of abuse do not come to anyone's attention in the first place and so will never go before a court because the person concerned may not realise that what they are experiencing is abuse. This could be the case where an adult has received support with their personal care all of their lives and they may, as a result, be very unclear about personal boundaries and about how they should be supported. We learn what is acceptable in terms of other people touching us as we grow up but some young people do not have the opportunity to meet their personal care needs without support. The result of this could be that as they never experience being self-reliant, they are unsure of boundaries in terms of personal space and dignity unless they are specifically taught them. This can be particularly an issue for people who are supported from childhood into adulthood but yet continue to be treated as if they were still a child.

2. Even if they do realise that a situation may be abusive or at the very least do not feel comfortable or safe about it, they may not have anyone who they trust to whom they can tell what has happened or is happening.

3. They may not have the language to be able to communicate their concerns, either due to an illness such as a stroke which has impeded their ability to speak, or they may be an adult with a learning disability with communication needs, which no-one they have contact with has the skill to meet.

4. They may be unwilling to complain or appear in court, even though they are able to state what has happened or is happening, either because they are afraid of the person who is abusing them or because that person might be a close family carer who they love or have close emotional ties to. This means that any reporting of any incidents just seems an impossibility to them. These complex situations often stop anyone else even being aware of possible abuse.

5. It may be the case that a person is being abused and is being prevented from having any access to people who might listen to or help them. They could be an older person living with relatives, possibly having sold their own home and given the money to those relatives.

6. Even if the suspicions or allegations are reported to someone, whether they go any further depends on the actions of the person they tell. They may not believe them and so not report the allegations to anyone else. They may know the alleged perpetrator and so decide not to report the allegation. They may not be clear about who they should talk to or they may have even made some misguided promise not to pass the information on to anyone else.

7. If the allegation is passed on and picked up for investigation by the local authority the outcome will then depend on internal decisions made and the skill and experience of the practitioners involved. The allegation may be of a sufficiently serious nature to warrant police involvement. However, there may be difficulties in the police gathering enough robust evidence for the Crown Prosecution Service (CPS) to be sufficiently confident of a successful outcome in court.

8. There may be difficulties in evidence in that the individual may be someone with dementia or a learning disability and may have difficulty in remembering names or sequences of events. In the case of someone with dementia, if the person is not always able to distinguish reality from non-reality, even though something may have taken place, without other evidence, it might be extremely difficult to prove or unravel from other non-related 'imaginings'.

It is for all of these reasons that the government has instructed local authorities to have procedures in relation to vulnerable adults. It is because some adults have great difficulty in accessing systems which are designed to ensure we all live in a civilised society. Vulnerable adults are often denied their rights as citizens of this country because of the reasons outlined above. Vulnerable adults are identified as such so they can receive the support they need to challenge exploitation or abuse whether that be through the courts or through other, non-legal means in an attempt to redress this balance.

Government strategies to address issues of adult abuse

The government has chosen to address the issue of adult abuse through a number of strategies. Firstly, through regulation, secondly through an attempt to enable vulnerable adults to access the criminal justice system more effectively and, thirdly, through providing a framework for agencies to develop more effective adult protection systems and to work more effectively together. Each of these strategies will now be examined, but the main emphasis will be on the third strategy.

Regulation

The foreword to *No Secrets* states that 'There can be no secrets and no hiding place when it comes to exposing the abuse of vulnerable adults'. It states that the Care Standards Act 2000 addresses the issues raised in the White Paper *Modernising Social Services* regarding the need to provide better protection to adults who need care and support. This is in recognition of the fact that many adults experience abuse or are subject to poor practice in the settings in which they receive services. The National Minimum Standards published under the Care Standards Act 2000 are an attempt to regulate and enforce conditions to ensure adults receive non-abusive and appropriate services. The regulations apply to settings which provide residential accommodation where people are supported with personal care needs. Unlike previous legislation, the regulations cover arrangements where a local authority acts as care provider.

The Commission for Social Care Inspection (CSCI) is the body which has regulatory responsibility for care homes, domiciliary care agencies, children's homes, residential family centres, nursing agencies, fostering agencies, voluntary adoption agencies, adoption support agencies, and adult placement schemes (Mandelstam, 2005, p. 515). In Wales, this function is carried out by the Care

Standards Inspectorate for Wales under the Care Standards Act 2000. In Scotland the responsible body is the Commission for the Regulation of Care under the Regulation of Care (Scotland) Act 2001 and in Northern Ireland, the Regulation and Improvement Authority will be the responsible body under the Health and Personal Social Services (Quality and Improvement and Regulation) (Northern Ireland) Order 2003 (Mandelstam, 2005, p. 513). The standards cover areas such as staffing issues including, for example, the suitability of the manager, employment checks and competency, experience and training of staff. It also covers issues relating to privacy and dignity of service users, restraint and the arrangements made to prevent service users being harmed, abused or put at risk. CSCI plays a crucial role in the prevention and detection of abusive situations and can be part of joint investigations with a local authority into alleged abuse taking place in the context of a residential placement.

Under the Care Standards Act 2000, there is a duty for the Secretary of State to keep a list of care workers who are deemed as unsuitable to work with vulnerable adults because they have either harmed or placed at risk of harm a vulnerable adult and the employer either has (or would have) dismissed them or transferred them to a non-care work role (Mandelstam, 2005, p. 405). This list is referred to as the POVA list (protection of vulnerable adults) and was started in July 2004. With the list come two duties for care providers. Firstly, to refer a care worker to it if they have harmed or placed at the risk of harm a vulnerable adult. Secondly, there is a duty to check new employees against the list as well as those employees who move from a non-care to a caring role within an agency. A person must not be employed if they are found to be on the POVA list. This regulation has been introduced following the recommendations of the Bichard Inquiry (2005) into the Soham murders where it was found that a system of sharing information about people who present a risk to children and vulnerable adults was needed.

Support in court processes

The second strategy of the government to address the issue of adult abuse is through the development of support for vulnerable adults if they appear as witnesses in relation to an alleged offence against them. The idea behind this is that some adults will be enabled to seek redress through the courts, as another citizen would. The practice of video interviewing children who have been abused to minimise the traumatic process of court appearances is fairly well established. This is a practice which is being increasingly applied to adults who would also find appearance in court too difficult and would be unable to obtain justice because of the court process rather than through it. 'Special measures' can be put in place for some vulnerable witnesses under The Youth Justice and Criminal Evidence Act 1999 (Mandelstam, 2005, p. 429). The idea of 'special measures' is that some aspects of the court experience can be changed with the purpose that the experience will be less intimidating or that some specific needs of the witness can be met in court. An appearance in court can be frightening and very stressful for anyone, but for some individuals, the whole process and environment makes it impossible for them to take part in the court hearing.

To be eligible for special measures, an adult must have a 'mental disorder' as defined in the Mental Health Act 1983 or have a significant impairment of intelligence or social functioning. The special measures can include the giving of evidence by a live link in court rather than being in the same court room as the accused, the removal of wigs and gowns, the use of video recorded evidence as well as the provision of communication aids.

A report can be provided to the court which can cover any area of the individual needs of the witness and how these might impact on the person's right to a fair hearing so that these needs can be addressed during the court process (Mandelstam, p. 429). For example, they might need language to be very simple, or questions repeated or allowed to have sufficient time to process what is actually being asked. This then means that if they are met by the court, then the witness is facilitated in receiving their rights to justice through the courts, which have been previously denied as the process was too complex and often anxiety provoking for vulnerable adults. These are important advances in the realm of adult protection. However, the difficulties involved for a person who has been subject to abuse and who may struggle to understand the court processes are not to be underestimated as they are considerable.

Policies for adult protection

The third strategy of the government and the one which is our chief concern here is the guidance given in relation to the policies and procedures to identify and address issues of adult abuse. I will first examine the *No Secrets* document as it still has relevance although *Safeguarding Adults* has built on it. The definition of abuse as defined in *No Secrets* is used in the later document. *No Secrets* defines abuse as 'a violation of an individual's human and civil rights by any other person or persons' (2.5). It adds that abuse can be a single act or repeated acts and states that the main types of abuse are: physical, sexual, psychological, financial or material, neglect or acts of omission and discriminatory abuse which includes racist or sexist abuse or that based on a person's disability (2.7). This means that abuse is viewed in terms of a violation of a person's human rights and recognition is given to the plethora of ways in which a person can have their human rights denied. *No Secrets* stated that the local authority social services departments should take the lead in 'inter-agency' collaboration to address issues of abuse. This is important as pieces of information are often known by different agencies but unless this information is shared, a whole picture cannot be ascertained and so mistakes can be made in deciding appropriate courses of action.

Safeguarding Adults, however, allows for different agencies to be responsible for co-ordinating investigations as will be seen below. It will probably take a number of years before this is true in reality and it is the principle that is important here, namely that all agencies should be involved in the collection of information and that they must work together with one agency taking responsibility for co-ordinating this. The *No Secrets* guidance adds a necessary note on the importance of confidentiality and the need for agencies to draw up a common agreement in relation to confidentiality and set out principles to govern the sharing of information in the interests of vulnerable adults (5.5).

No Secrets proposes a framework on which local authorities can base their own procedures. The guidance suggests factors to be taken into consideration when deciding on the seriousness of abuse:

- the **vulnerability** of the individual;
- the **nature and extent** of the abuse;
- the **length of time** it has been occurring;
- the **impact** on the individual; and
- the risk of **repeated or increasingly serious** acts involving this or other vulnerable adults. (2.19).

There is obviously a need for a lot of information to be known about an individual before the questions above can be answered, which can be very complex and involves a lot of skilled work with a number of professionals. One example of this would be if the person has complex communication needs. A speech and language therapist can either work directly with them or provide advice to the social worker and police on how best to interview somebody with these needs. This joint working to meet the needs of the individual not only supports them in the process, but retrieves best evidence and so increases the likelihood of a successful outcome in court. A balance has to be found on the most appropriate way to support a person in such a way that does not make the whole experience intolerable for them. Too many professionals working with an individual can just be bewildering for them. This, again, has to be balanced with how best to support them and give them the opportunity to be listened to and understood. An advocate may be appropriate as they can help the person negotiate how they are worked with.

It is apparent that an assessment is required to ascertain what the person has been experiencing and the impact this has had on them. The guidance suggests a process of assessment to evaluate the following:

- Is the person suffering harm or exploitation?
- Does the person suffering or causing harm/exploitation meet the NHS and Community Care Act (1990) eligibility criteria?

- Is the intervention in the best interests of the vulnerable adult fitting the criteria and/or in the public interest?
- Does the assessment account for the depth and conviction of the feelings of the person alleging the abuse? (*No Secrets*, 2.20)

The second question highlights the fact that the local authority may have a duty towards the alleged perpetrator as well as the alleged victim of abuse if they also are in need of community care services under the NHSCCA. This may be the case if the alleged abuse has taken place in a residential setting or within a day services environment, for example. It is important that the needs of both the alleged victim and the alleged perpetrator are taken into account and that a clear plan of action is identified for both adults in terms of how they are to be worked with.

The third question seems to apply to the victim as well as the perpetrator, if they are also a vulnerable adult in that they meet the criteria for community care services and may be unable to take care of or protect themselves. This can lead to very difficult decisions in relation to any possible intervention being in the best interests of both parties. An example of this might be whether both adults should continue to attend the same day service. Strong feelings can be evoked from the individuals concerned and often their families and the workers who work with them. It takes very skilled judgment to ascertain the 'best' course of action, and highlights the need for a thorough assessment of the needs of both individuals as well as the circumstances of the alleged abuse. However, under the *Safeguarding Adults* definition of a vulnerable adult, they may not be at risk of their independence due to abuse or neglect in that particular instance. The principle still applies though, that they will need to be supported in an appropriate way and have a plan in their own right.

The fourth question is relevant in any decision-making process. It is important that the alleged victim be supported to state their wishes clearly. This applies equally to both the investigation and decision-making process. Inclusion of the adult in any case conference is good practice but if this is inappropriate or against the wishes of the individual, it is essential that they are represented in such a way that is accurate and in accordance with their wishes. *Safeguarding Adults* formalises this as good practice by stating that if the adult has capacity, then they must be informed and in agreement with a referral about any concerns unless there are 'overriding public duties to act or gaining consent would put the person at further risk' (9.4.3). *Safeguarding Adults* states that an adult who has mental capacity and who is the subject of an investigation should be included as a 'full partner' (9.6.7) in the strategy discussion and this might include the use of an advocate or victim support services to support the person. Where it is not possible to include the adult in the actual discussion, they are to be included as fully as possible in the decision-making process and agreement with the adult on how to include their views should be sought by the 'safeguarding manager' (see below).

Inter-agency working

No Secrets sets out the expectation that agencies will work together and that inter-agency policies will be developed to facilitate this. *Safeguarding Adults* identifies this as a foundational principle, but also sets out expectations in terms of what each stage of the process will be called. The reason for this is that the discretion previously given to local authorities has led to confusion, especially with agencies working with more than one local authority.

Section 4 of *No Secrets* sets out the principles which agencies should adhere to. These principles are worth examining here as they make a number of important points.

1. Agencies should 'actively promote the empowerment and well-being of vulnerable adults through the services they provide' (4.3 ii). This means that services should not only be non-abusive but should provide and actively work to create an environment in which adults are listened to and taken seriously.

2. Agencies should 'act in a way which supports the rights of the individual to lead an independent life based on self-determination and personal choice' (4.3 iii). In order to achieve this, workers within agencies have to believe that all people have rights, including the right to make choices which may not be the choices they themselves would make. I would strongly maintain that it is impossible to support people in leading lives which are lived in the way they would want to lead them, without having a fundamental belief in their right to such a life.

This does not mean ignoring all issues which need to be taken account of, but working with people in such a way that support and risk issues are addressed together, so that people are enabled to exercise choice over their own lives.

3. Agencies should 'recognise people who are unable to take their own decisions and/or to protect themselves, their assets and bodily integrity' (4.3 iv). The issue of capacity has already been examined and will be further discussed later in the book as it is a vital one, but the principles recognise that there are indeed people who, for a variety of reasons, are unable to make their own decisions. The challenge for workers in this case is to decide what the best course of action for an individual is, how to take forward any possible abuse investigation, and what the person might want were they able to make a decision. Possible options for legal interventions will be examined later in this chapter in the case of capacity issues.

4. Agencies should 'recognise that the right to self-determination can involve risk and ensure that such risk is recognised and understood by all concerned, and minimised whenever possible'; it adds 'there should be an open discussion between the individual and the agencies about the risks involved to him or her' (4.3 v). This is really important as a poorly thought through approach to risk management can result in harmful situations for some adults. It is vital that the belief in service users' right to lead their lives in accordance with their own choices

is informed by a careful assessment of any risk issues and that these are addressed in a honest and measured way with the adult concerned as far as this is possible and in a way in which they can understand. The challenge to workers within the agencies is to decide how to achieve this. One approach may work with one individual but not with another. It is important that the communication needs of individuals are carefully considered and the most appropriate way of including them in any discussions regarding risk issues is identified. This calls for careful planning and a discussion with the person concerned as well as those who know them best, be that other workers or family members. The guidance calls for strategies, policies and services to be integrated within the legislative framework to ensure the safety of vulnerable adults (4.3 vi).

5. Agencies should 'ensure that when the right to an independent lifestyle and choice is at risk, the individual concerned receives appropriate help, including advice, protection and support from relevant agencies' (4.3 vii).

6. Lastly, agencies should 'ensure that the law and statutory requirements are known and used appropriately so that vulnerable adults receive the protection of the law and access to the judicial process' (4.3 viii).

These last two principles emphasise that the agencies have a role in supporting people in an independent lifestyle, but when that is threatened as a result of abuse, they have the responsibility to support the adult in addressing the wrong done to them through accessing the legal system if this is appropriate. These principles, taken together, demonstrate the importance of an approach which is active in working in a way which is not only non-oppressive but which respects the rights of the people being supported. An approach is needed which supports the adults in the lifestyle of their choice and in a way that addresses issues of risk with them and supports them in seeking redress if their rights are violated.

Responsibility to act if abuse is suspected

No Secrets sets out principles for the investigation of possible adult abuse whereas Safeguarding Adults gives an actual framework to be followed. Both documents are clear on the responsibility of any worker who is alerted to possible abuse and it is important that all workers are familiar with the role they might play in an investigation into suspected or alleged abuse. The guidance is very clear on the responsibility of any worker to act on any suspicion or evidence of abuse or neglect and to pass on their concerns to the responsible person or agency.

It is not the role of a worker in day services, housing, a residential setting or any other setting where services are provided, to make a judgment about what is being alleged, nor to investigate the allegations, but to pass the concern on to the appropriate person.

If this is your role, you should be aware of who you need to contact in such an eventuality as uncertainty on this point could cause delays or even mean that something is not reported. If you work directly with adults, you are perhaps the most likely person to hear of or see something which gives rise to suspicion and therefore you have a key role. It is not possible to over-emphasise its importance or to over-estimate the harm which can be done if you ignore concerns. It can be very difficult to report a concern if it implicates a colleague or maybe a family member with whom you have built up a good relationship. However, the guidance is clear that you have a responsibility to report concerns.

What to do if you are alerted to the possibility of abuse

If you are a worker supporting a vulnerable adult and you are alerted to a possible abusive situation by a vulnerable adult disclosing information to you, what do you do? *Safeguarding Adults* offers good practice advice for workers who may be alerted to possible abuse through a disclosure:

- Remaining calm and not showing shock or disbelief.
- Listening carefully to what is being said.
- Not asking detailed or probing questions.
- Demonstrating a sympathetic approach by acknowledging regret and concern that what has been reported has happened.
- Ensuring that any emergency action needed has been taken.
- Confirming that the information will be treated seriously.
- Giving them information about the steps that will be taken.
- Informing them that they will receive feedback as to the result of the concerns they have raised and from whom.
- Giving the person contact details so they can report any further issues or ask any questions that may arise. (9.3.7)

What is clear from this practice guidance is that you should be prepared for the eventuality of having a disclosure made to you. You should already be familiar with the steps that will be taken and how that will be fed back to the person who is the subject of the concerns. The list gives the impression of someone who is well informed, responsive, sympathetic and skilful in their response, especially in the appropriate level of their response.

The importance of not asking detailed or probing questions is high-lighted as this is not your role if you are the person who is initially alerted to possible abuse, but will be the role of whoever carries out a 'safeguarding assessment' or carries out an abuse investigation as it may be termed.

This key role played right at the very beginning of concerns being expressed highlights the importance of you being well trained, responsible and skilful.

What happens once the concern is reported?

Once a concern is reported, the *No Secrets* guidance lays out objectives for any subsequent investigation. Facts have to be established, an assessment has to be made of the needs of the vulnerable adult for 'protection, support and redress' and decisions have to be made 'with regard to what follow-up action should be taken with regard to the perpetrator and the service or its management if they have been culpable, ineffective or negligent' (6.3). Depending on the findings of the investigation, the guidance says resulting actions might be 'primarily supportive or therapeutic or it might involve the application of sanctions, suspension, regulatory activity or criminal prosecution or disciplinary action . . .' (6.4). The investigation may involve joint working with the police if a criminal offence is being alleged and be a straightforward and fairly quick piece of work or it could be very complex, involving many professionals and court work.

Safeguarding Adults

Safeguarding Adults sets out 11 sets of good practice standards for adult protection work, which build on the guidance from *No Secrets* and the experience of workers involved in adult protection work. This puts a lot of the principles outlined in *No Secrets* into the form of standards which, when followed, are designed to develop consistent, high quality adult protection work.

As already stated, the implementation of *Safeguarding Adults* will probably take a number of years and different services will be at different stages in their adoption of its recommendations. Regardless of where your area is in terms of its implementation, it is important to consider the principles outlined in it and to view local practice in the light of its messages. It acknowledges the contentious nature of the term 'vulnerable adults' as it can be misunderstood 'because it seems to locate the cause of abuse with the victim, rather than placing responsibility with the actions or omissions of others' (p. 4). The document also points to significant legal and policy changes which have taken place in adult social and health care since *No Secrets*, accompanied by a 're-focusing of its language and philosophy' (p. 5). It pinpoints *Fair Access to Care Services* (FACS) (DoH, 2002), as of particular significance.

The FACS guidance sets out the criteria for eligibility to services and has as the key criterion for determining services 'risk to independence and well-being'. According to *Safeguarding Adults*, this means that the concept of a 'vulnerable adult' is replaced by 'an assessment of risk posed by the abuse and neglect to the quality of life of the individual adult concerned' (p. 5). The document states that 'the emphasis is now on supporting adults to access services of their own choosing, rather than "stepping in" to provide protection'. This is to be seen alongside a clear duty to provide protection to those who lack mental capacity. What this seems to mean in practice is that adults are regarded as citizens and the promotion of their rights, including the right to live a life free of abuse, is seen as the task of all who work with adults who access community care services.

The new term 'Safeguarding Adults' is to be used in place of protecting 'vulnerable adults' or 'adult protection' work. Again, this change in language and emphasis may be at different points in different areas. The important principle is that it makes the responsibility of 'safeguarding' adults the role of all who work with adults who are eligible for community services rather than it just being the role of a few workers to provide adult protection services. Never before has the real importance of the role of all who work with adults been highlighted so clearly. If you work with adults who are eligible for community care services, you have a role in 'safeguarding' them. This is not an option but is an integral and essential part of your role.

Adults in a victimising society

'Safeguarding Adults' procedures are to be a 'local area-based, multi-agency response which is made to every adult *"who is or may be eligible for community care services"* (National Health Service and Community Care Act 1990) **and** whose independence and well-being is at risk due to abuse or neglect' (*Safeguarding Adults*, p. 5). This is a welcome development in thinking as it does put the development of services in the context of human rights and citizenship. It also shows how the old term 'vulnerable adult' stigmatised the adult concerned. However, I would argue that this new language still does not go far enough and I will argue this more fully later in the book. I would want the language to reflect the oppression experienced by some adults and so would maintain that 'adults in a victimising society' more accurately reflects the experience of many adults.

I fully endorse the approach which aims to provide services that encourage adults to enjoy their rights as citizens and which seeks to support those who lack capacity to access protection. The reality for many adults is that the culture where they live, receive day services, care, support or a short break is such that they are not treated as equal citizens and so the fact that they have mental capacity or not is not really the issue. If an adult is living in an environment where they are subject to humiliating treatment, it is that very environment which needs to be challenged, not just in relation to one particular adult, but as a whole. If one adult is victimised, the chance is that others are too. This is indeed recognised in the guidance and Standards three and four are concerned with the prevention of abuse and neglect in the community and within service delivery respectively. The guidance talks of the 'increased vulnerability' (p. 13) of some adults to abuse and identifies the following as reasons for this:

- Lack of inclusion in protective social networks, including education and employment.

- Dependency on others (who may misuse their position) for vital needs including mobility, access to information and control of finances.
- Lack of access to remedies for abuse and neglect.
- Social acceptability of low standards for care and treatment.
- Social acceptability of domestic abuse.
- Dynamics of power within institutional care settings.

The guidance stresses the importance of local forums, planning processes and services being accessible to people covered by the policy, particularly those relating to crime and disorder, regeneration and health and well-being. This is key to the whole approach of the policy, namely that freedom from abuse is achieved through accessing and realising citizenship rights. To address the concern of people who may pose a risk to others and are themselves covered by the policy, a plan is to be drawn up under the Multi-Agency Protection Panel Arrangements (MAPPA). Also, under the *Safeguarding Adults* guidance, multi-agency protocols for a 'Safeguarding Adults' serious case review should be agreed. Multi-agency policies are to detail the stages of an investigation and give clear timescales for each stage.

Any suspected abuse has to be reported immediately and a referral made the same day 'into a multi-agency context'. A decision has to be then made by the end of the next day on whether or not to use the 'Safeguarding Adults' procedures for the concern. If the procedures are deemed to be appropriate, then a 'Safeguarding assessment strategy', which is a plan for assessing risk and addressing any immediate concerns, is to be completed within five working days. Following this, a 'Safeguarding assessment' is to be completed to determine if abuse is likely to have occurred within four weeks of the referral. A 'Safeguarding plan' is to be formulated which will co-ordinate a multi-agency response to the risk of abuse that has been identified within a further four weeks. The whole process has to be reviewed within six months and annually after that. The responsibility for co-ordinating multi-agency working together is that of the 'safeguarding manager' and this person may be employed by any of the partner agencies, but they must have appropriate levels of experience and skill for this role. Such a person would be acting on behalf of the 'Safeguarding Adults' partnership and will be accountable to it via their agency.

As has already been noted, statutory agencies historically have taken the lead responsibility for co-ordinating abuse investigations but it is anticipated in *Safeguarding Adults* that other agencies could also take on the co-ordinating role. This would be decided on a case-by-case basis and obviously with agreement between all the agencies involved in any particular investigation. This would need to be agreed right at the beginning of any investigation.

Whistle blowing

If there are concerns of abuse in relation to your agency and there are clear reasons why you are unable to raise them within the agency, then you should follow whistle-blowing procedures. Your agency should have a procedure in place detailing who to contact if you are unable to take up the concerns directly. The Public Interest Disclosure Act which was introduced in 1999 was designed to assist whistle-blowers. The Act expects that employers should develop procedures which name a nominated person to whom concerns can be directed and who is not necessarily in the agency. Any concerns would be of the nature of a person being harmed, having been harmed in the past or in danger of being harmed. If the concerns are reported in line with the legislation, then you will be free from the employers taking action such as termination of your employment.

Confidentiality

In the context of safeguarding adults, confidentiality is important for three reasons.

Firstly, it shows respect to adults if the information they give us or we know about them is treated with the same care as we would want any information about ourselves to be. This is important as it reflects an attitude of respect and is part of providing a service which values people as citizens rather than treats them as having fewer rights than other people.

Secondly, you need to be clear regarding your responsibility in the case of adult protection issues as there can be circumstances where confidentiality may have to be broken to prevent harm to someone.

Thirdly, you have responsibilities in regard to agency policies in terms of confidentiality and you must be clear about what these are.

Confidentiality seems to be a concept that people either take scant regard of or are really unsure about what it means in practice. I have often heard care workers in a supermarket queue openly discussing the personal care details of adults they are supporting. This is a blatant disregard of confidentiality. Other workers perhaps wouldn't dream of doing this, but might openly discuss people and their personal information in a communal kitchen or in a stairway or thoroughfare. These are also breaches of confidentiality and do not show the respect to the adults we support that they either deserve or are entitled to.

Confidentiality is enshrined in law and so any breaches are not only a matter of poor practice. English common law recognises the concept of a confidential relationship and the duty of confidence. The Data Protection Act 1998 and the Human Rights Act 1998 have introduced enforceable rights for service users about how the information they provide workers with is used. Professional groups have their own codes of practice or ethics which incorporate confidentiality. I have based the following guidelines on the BASW (British Association of Social Workers) *The Code of Ethics for Social Work* (1975) as it provides a useful framework, but there are other codes which also have helpful guidelines.

Confidential information

There might arise a situation where you are privy to information about an adult you are supporting, for example in relation to a risk of a particular behaviour which could injure someone else. You must:

> Divulge confidential information only with the consent of the service user . . . , except where there is clear evidence of serious risk to the service user, worker, other persons or the community, or in other circumstances judged exceptional on the basis of professional consideration and consultation, limiting any such breach of confidence to the needs of the situation at the time. (p. 10, 4.1. 7 (d))

In other words, every effort should be made to gain the permission of the adult first, but if for some reason this is not possible, then information which could prevent someone getting injured can be shared without permission, although only in that circumstance. Such a situation would always warrant a conversation with a manager as the decision to share information without consent is not to be taken lightly.

Records

Confidential information is recorded on a routine basis in files or on electronic systems. While this is essential so that needs can be met and workers are accountable for their actions, this also means that care has to be taken with who has access to information. Workers must:

> Ensure, so far as it is in their power, that records, whether manual or electronic are stored securely, are protected from unauthorised access, and are not transferred, manually or electronically, to locations where access may not be strictly controlled. (p. 10, 4.1.7 (f))

Workers must:

> Record information impartially and accurately, recording only relevant matters and specifying the source of information. (p. 10, 4.1.7 (g))

When information must be shared

There are some instances when you will have a duty to share information and this duty will override confidentiality. Information has to be shared if the information is needed in order to protect a child at risk of significant harm as defined by the Children Act 1989, to protect the public from acts of terrorism, as a duty to the courts or under the Drug Trafficking Offences Act 1986. However, it is still good practice to discuss this with the adult about whom you are concerned unless to do so would put others at risk.

Where information is known that could prevent or detect a crime, public bodies have the power but not the duty to disclose information (Section 115 of the Crime and Disorder Act 1998).

There can be a conflict between confidentiality and inter-agency information sharing and this needs to be addressed in a coherent fashion. There are principles, such as those already outlined about risk to the individual or others and clear duties as outlined above. However, some cases are not as clear-cut and any decisions taken will have to be carefully recorded, together with the reasons why were they taken and any individuals consulted.

Issues of staff training

As safeguarding adults is seen as the role of all who work with adults and includes providing a non-abusive service as well as recognising signs of abuse, the guidance sets out standards for training for all staff. This would include recognition of abuse and neglect, the potential for its occurrence as well as awareness of *Safeguarding Adults* procedures and the requirement of reporting concerns as well as agency arrangements for reporting such concerns (*Safeguarding Adults*, 5.9).

Agencies working in partnership

Like *No Secrets*, *Safeguarding Adults* stresses the importance of a multi-agency partnership and calls it the 'Safeguarding Adults partnership'. These partnerships are important for information sharing which is vital as inquiries into adult deaths through neglect have identified that greater information sharing and multi-agency work together might have placed the agencies in a position to safeguard the adult concerned. The tragic death of Beverley Lewis is one such case. Beverley was a 23 year old young woman who would have qualified as a vulnerable adult. Beverley died as a result of pneumonia compounded by emaciation. She had been living with her mother. Beverley weighed just 3 stone 13 lbs when she died, had not left the house for many years before her death and was found surrounded by newspapers, hoarded food and street refuse. Her mother had mental health needs and was hostile to any professionals who tried to visit Beverley and herself. Gloucestershire Social Services and Health Authority were heavily criticised for failing to prevent the tragedy. Poor co-ordination of services was identified as being a key factor in Beverley's death. A co-ordinated sharing of information, agreed plans and interventions may well have saved Beverley (Lamb, 2000). This was obviously a complex situation to work with and to progress, as it is difficult to work with people who are hostile and who deny access to professionals. However, in these very difficult cases the need for co-ordinated working is even more vital as a plan can be formulated based on shared information and professionals can work together to address issues.

Issues of mental capacity

Safeguarding Adults states that in line with the Mental Capacity Act 2005, the procedures should be based on the presumption of capacity, and on the right of adults to make choices, even if these are deemed by others to be unwise. This principle should be applied to situations in relation to abuse or neglect. This is often a very difficult area for workers to come to an understanding of, as it can be challenging to work with an adult who is choosing to put themselves at some kind of risk. Examples of this may be people who choose to stay in an abusive relationship or who put themselves at risk in terms of sexual exploitation or choosing to mix with those who it is clear to an observer have a destructive influence on the adult. The guidance is clear that capacity about decisions includes having information about what is taking place, any resulting harm and the options that are open to stop the abuse or reduce the harm. Capacity includes the ability to weigh up the information and to communicate a decision. However, where an adult does choose to live with a risk of abuse, then a 'safeguarding plan' should be drawn up to include details of services to minimise the risk.

The importance of ensuring that the adult is not being intimidated into a decision is highlighted in, for example, a decision to stay with an abusive partner. This necessitates a skilful and thoughtful approach on the part of any one working with an adult who chooses to live with a degree of risk in terms of abuse. It is not to be taken as guaranteed that, even if an adult can communicate a clear wish, they have a clear understanding of the issues involved in their situation. Work with and support to the adult may be appropriate to ensure they have an understanding of the context in which they have made their decision. An example might be a woman who is choosing to put herself at risk in some way because of her belief that men have more rights than women due to the sexism which she has experienced and which has shaped her understanding of herself in a very negative way. It would certainly be appropriate to challenge her understanding and to support her in gaining a new understanding of her right to be respected as a woman and not to be subjected to degrading treatment at the hands of some men.

The rights of the adult and their capacity to make decisions are fundamental to the *Safeguarding Adults* philosophy. When a person is deemed not to have the capacity to make decisions about protection from abuse, then the guidance states that 'action should be taken to protect them'. It qualifies this by the statement 'Any such action must be proportionate to the level of risk and take any knowledge of the person's previously expressed wishes into account' (6.8). This would involve the procedures as already outlined but without including the adult as a full partner. The reference to 'previously expressed wishes' is in accordance with the Mental Capacity Act's concept of capacity being a changeable quality.

An example of this would be if an older person with dementia was now unable to express their view of care they were receiving from a partner, having previously stated a firm wish to stay with this partner. This would clearly be a relevant factor to consider. However, in such a case a view might also be held that, as the partner had not been abusive before, the situation is different now since the older person hadn't been able to take any experience of abuse into account when they stated their wishes previously. Such judgments require a really careful and thoughtful approach and one which is based on a desire to maximise the person's realisation of their rights as citizens.

What happens if an adult has been abused?

If, after a careful consideration of all the information gathered as part of the safeguarding assessment, the conclusion is reached that an adult has been abused, what can be done about the situation? This will depend on what has taken place, what the views are of the person who has been abused, if they are able to state them, and who has been the abuser.

If the abuse took place in a setting which is registered under CSCI, then they will have had a role in any investigation and if it was in relation to a standard that they inspect against, they can make recommendations and targets for the establishment to improve its practice. It may mean that disciplinary action is taken against an employee, resulting in possible job loss if the abuse is of a serious nature or that a member of staff receives training in an area of their practice. It rather depends on what has happened. Certainly there are some actions which are beyond poor practice and which are clearly abusive.

There are some actions which are now an illegal act, whereas until recently they were not covered by the law. Rape and sexual assault have obviously been covered by the law as they are criminal acts; however, the Sexual Offences Act 2003 reformed the law on sexual offences. It made a number of acts offences if they are committed with a person with a 'mental disorder'. 'Mental disorder' is defined by the Mental Health Act 1983 Section 1 as 'mental illness, arrested or incomplete development of mind, psychopathic disorder and any other disorder or disability of mind'. If a person is unable to refuse the sexual activity due to lack of capacity to either understand the activity or the consequences of it or if the person cannot communicate their choice due to 'mental disorder' and if the perpetrator knows of the lack of capacity or the inability to communicate, then the act is an offence.

The Act details four offences under sections 30-33:

1. sexual activity with a mentally disordered person;
2. causing or inciting a person with a mental disorder to engage in sexual activity;
3. engaging in sexual activity in the presence of a person with a mental disorder for the purpose of sexual gratification of the perpetrator; and

4. causing a person with a mental disorder to watch a sexual act for the purpose of sexual gratification of the perpetrator.

Another set of offences is outlined in the Act which specifically relates to care workers. The offences are the same as the four listed above, but do not rely on the inability of the victim to refuse, so consent is not an issue in these cases. The only circumstances in which it is not an offence for a care worker to have a sexual relationship with a 'mentally disordered person' is when they are married or where a sexual relationship existed immediately prior to the person taking up the role of a care worker. This means that any such offences are now covered by the judicial process and care workers who commit such offences should be prosecuted through the courts.

Incidents such as assault or theft from an individual should also be dealt with through the courts and the police should be involved at the outset in any such investigation. I have already mentioned the issues for witnesses in the court system as justice is not always obtained where a person is not able to state their case in a court environment.

Options for intervention when a person lacks mental capacity

If a person is deemed to lack capacity and is clearly unable to express a view on their abusive situation, then what options are available in terms of intervention?

1. Services or support that could prevent abuse

There are services which could be commissioned which might alleviate a stressful situation for carers and so improve the situation and that could be enough to prevent further abuse or neglect. A carer is entitled to a carer's assessment in their own right and services provided under the Carers and Disabled Children Act 2000 might be sufficient to address any issues. An example of a service that could help carers is a short break for the person they are caring for, giving them some free time away from caring responsibilities. No specific new legislation was passed at the time of *No Secrets* to accompany it, as Mandelstam (2005) has observed:

> local social services adult protection work primarily . . . rests on the existing community care legislation. (p. 404)

Mandelstam cites an adult protection case concerning an assisted suicide where a judge acknowledges *No Secrets* guidance but held that a local authority's duties were limited to addressing the community care needs of the particular person as assessed by the authority (p. 404). In other words, *No Secrets* is set in the context of legislation which directs workers in relation to assessing the need for community care services rather than providing a framework for intervention such as can be seen in the Children Act 1989.

What can happen is that workers seem to get 'stuck' about knowing how to proceed with situations which can be very complex. The value of the procedures as set out in *Safeguarding Adults* is that any worker should not be left to flounder in uncertainty, but a clear strategy should be agreed on how to proceed with a situation and a case conference convened to formulate a plan. The fact that there is a process to follow should provide a framework in which decisions can be made jointly with other professionals rather than one worker being left to decide how to proceed. Although there is not one piece of legislation which outlines how to proceed in circumstances of abuse, there are options which are available to be used and should be considered where applicable as part of any plan.

2. Declaratory relief

One option available is that of *declaratory relief*. This is based on the common-law 'doctrine of necessity', in which it is deemed lawful to intervene in a person's life for their protection in a situation where they are unable to express a view. Declaratory relief is not an adult protection intervention, but can be used as such. An example of an action being legal due to the doctrine of necessity, which is not in relation to adult protection but illustrates its nature, is if life saving first aid was administered without a person's permission if they were unconscious, so unable to consent. Clearly, it would be illegal to administer an intrusive procedure without their permission, but because they are unable to consent, the procedure can legally be administered as it is in their interest. Declaratory relief is a legal intervention available due to the same principle, namely, that it is intervening in a person's life for their benefit when they are unable to give consent, but in this case due to lack of capacity.

Declaratory relief can be sought in situations where, for example, the person lives with their family and an assessment has identified that the person is being abused but they are unable to protect themselves or express a view as to what should happen by way of intervention in their life. An application can be made to the court for direction in specific circumstances such as where a person should live. This direction, which has to come from a High Court judge, can be gained very quickly, so is attractive in circumstances where urgency is required. The judge can base their decision on the initial information supplied and the case will then be heard in court. This means that action can be taken, for example in relation to where the person lives, immediately and prior to any full court hearing. The proceedings in these cases are complex, lengthy and expensive, but do provide a real option for intervention where other options have been explored and have proved impossible. Obviously, working in partnership with and supporting the family and the adult is the preferable option, but there are some situations where the family or carers are either abusive or negligent and display an unwillingness or inability to work with agencies. The case of Beverley Lewis cited earlier might have been an appropriate case for an application for declaratory relief.

3. Cases of self-neglect

Although self-neglect is not always covered in agency policies about abuse, there may be occasions when an adult is living in a state of severe self-neglect and may even be posing a risk to others. If such a situation seems to warrant the removal of the person from their own home to a form of care setting, then this can be accomplished under section 47 of the National Assistance Act 1948. Under this section, a local authority can obtain a magistrate's order to remove a person from their home providing they meet the criteria, which is that they 'are suffering from grave chronic disease or, being aged, infirm or physically incapacitated, are living in insanitary conditions; and are unable to devote to themselves, and are not receiving from other persons, proper care and attention'.

There are some safeguards with this in terms of notice being given to the individual and agreement by a medical officer that this course of action is necessary for their own safety and well-being, or that they are posing a risk to others. Under this Act, mental capacity is not an issue as it can be used regardless of whether someone has capacity or not. However, this is a very 'heavy-handed' action and is therefore not used very often. It is not clear whether an action of this nature would be contrary to the Human Rights Act 1998 although I rather suspect it would be.

The fact that this may be considered highlights the difficult decisions which sometimes have to be made in terms of balancing a person's rights with the risks that they may pose to themselves which could result in the loss of their own life. These are very difficult decisions to make when working with an individual in such circumstances. What is vital is that all decision-making takes full account of a person's rights.

4. Mental Health Act 1983

When a person might be thought to be posing a threat to their own or others safety, there are instances where the provision of services after an assessment under the NHS and Community Care Act 1990, are not deemed to be sufficient to prevent this harm as the threat might be thought to be caused by mental health needs. In such cases, social services departments have a duty under the Mental Health Act 1983.

One of these duties would be to consider a possible admission to a hospital for assessment and possibly treatment of their mental health needs. In such circumstances an Approved Social Worker (ASW) needs to complete an assessment and be in agreement with the General Practitioner and a Psychiatrist that a stay in hospital is the most appropriate way of meeting the person's mental health needs and addressing the issues identified in the assessment.

The important principle here is that the least restrictive course of action that will alleviate the situation is pursued. It may be that the person has sufficient insight to agree that they need support in a hospital and will therefore agree to a voluntary admission. This is always preferable to a compulsory detention. Even if it is agreed that they need to be detained against their will in order to prevent them hurting themselves or someone else, this should be done in a way that is as empowering as possible. This sounds like a real contradiction as when an individual is detained under the Mental Health Act 1983, then by definition they are deprived of their liberty. How then can there be any possibility of empowerment under such drastic circumstances? I think there are still ways of working with a person which makes the process for them more empowering than it otherwise might be. Someone in such a situation should still be treated with the utmost respect and dignity and informed of what is happening and why, with the implications of their situation explained to them in such a way that they can understand. Any timescales should be explained as well as the process of appeal and how and when their case will be reviewed and by whom. It might not be appropriate to give this information all at once as the person may be unable to understand it all or remember it as the process can be a very traumatic one. Time should not only be taken to explain what is happening but it should also be spent at the right point where they are receptive to what is being said to them.

The Mental Health Act 1983 stipulates the grounds for compulsory admission to hospital as:

1. that they are, or may be, mentally disordered;
2. that they ought to be detained in the interests of their own health or safety, or with a view to the protection of other persons. (Section 2(2), Mental Health Act 1983)

Both of these criteria must be met and it is medical staff who must provide recommendations in relation to the first criteria. A doctor cannot apply for an individual to be detained: this is done either by the ASW or by the 'nearest relative'.

A person might be detained under Section 2 of the Mental Health Act 1983, which allows them to be assessed, or assessed and then treated. They can be detained initially for 28 days under this Section, during which time a decision will have to be made in relation to continuing care. At the end of the time, they could be discharged, remain as an informal patient or be detained under Section 3. A person can be detained under Section 3 for up to six months and this is renewable. In order to be detained under Section 3, an individual has to be assessed as having a form of 'mental disorder' as defined in section 1 of the Act:

'Mental disorder' means mental illness, arrested or incomplete development of mind, psychopathic disorders and any other disorder or disability of mind and 'mentally disordered' shall be considered accordingly. (Section 1(2) Mental Health Act 1983)

The same principle applies to a person continuing to be detained in hospital as admitted in the first place, namely that this is the only course of action available and that the treatment can only take place in hospital. Although a person who is detained in hospital is unable to enjoy their rights as citizens as they have been deprived of their liberty, I would argue that this makes it even more important to consider the way they are treated and spoken to while they are in hospital. The most depressing places I have ever been to have been hospitals where people have been detained under the Mental Health Act 1983. These can obviously be very difficult places to work and I do not want to minimise the skill required to work in such an environment. However, I think that sometimes the very culture of the hospital can be anything but conducive to any sort of recovery of the person detained. The actual buildings can be drab and have a generally unkempt appearance. Staff can talk in very negative terms, both of the work that they do and the people they work with. It is a reality that sometimes staff members get demoralised and exhausted, but it is so important that the organisational practices and attitudes of staff members are thoughtfully examined. Questions that should be asked of practices in such settings are:

1. Why are they there?
2. Are they really necessary?
3. Do they help or hinder people in their recovery?

In an environment in which people are detained, it is still possible to treat them with respect and listen to their concerns. This would seem to be essential if people are to recover.

National Service Framework

The National Service Framework (NSF) for Mental Health (DoH, 1999a) contains standards which should be applied to the provision of services for people with mental health needs. It refers to people on the Care Programme Approach, which is a system designed to ensure people are appropriately assessed, receive a care plan, are assigned a key worker and are regularly reviewed.

The standards of the NSF, if followed, should address some of the issues of how people are treated when they are detained under the Mental Health Act 1983.

Each adult in that situation should have 'timely access to an appropriate (hospital) bed, which is in the least restrictive environment consistent with self and public protection, and is as close to home as possible' (Standard 2). The emphasis is on the reduction of risk of harm to the person as well as members of the public which would be expected, as these would be the criteria for being detained in the first place. This is an important principle as an environment that is too restrictive and is not warranted by the level of risk someone presents to themselves or others could be detrimental to the psychological well-being of that person.

Any professional, however, who has been trying to find a bed for a person who is to be detained under the Mental Health Act 1983, will know that there is not a huge choice. This makes the attitude of the staff working in such units all the more important. The adult who has been admitted may not be in an ideal environment to meet their needs. A considered and respectful approach from staff is vital as is the promotion of a culture which values the people who are detained and seeks to minimise their distress.

5. Neglect

It is an exciting time for adult protection work as legislation seems to be reflecting a growing awareness in this vital area. It is an offence, therefore, for employees or managers of a hospital to ill-treat or wilfully neglect a 'mentally disordered' patient receiving treatment as either an in-patient or an out-patient (Mandelstam, 2005, p. 426). It is also an offence to ill-treat or wilfully neglect an individual on a Guardianship Order or someone who is subject to supervision for aftercare under the Mental Health Act 1983. Recent legislation has broadened the scope of offences against vulnerable adults. Under the Mental Capacity Act 2005, it is an offence for a carer to ill-treat or neglect a person who lacks capacity. Causing the death of a vulnerable adult will be introduced as an offence under the Domestic Violence, Crime and Victims Act 2004. This Act concerns circumstances where the death is caused by a person or people from the same household as the victim.

Assessments, care plans and reviews

There are processes which are designed to safeguard adults which I have already detailed in Chapter 3. However, there are other processes which I would argue should be an essential part of providing an environment where people are supported to enjoy their rights and be free from harm of any kind. These processes are assessing, care planning and reviewing. Every person who supports an adult in any way should contribute to or be informed by these processes, which includes any unpaid carers. Under The NHS and Community Care Act 1990, statutory agencies have a duty to assess adults who 'appear to be in need of community care services' (Section 47 (1)).

Assessments and person centred planning

It is vital that such assessments accurately identify the needs of individuals so that agencies providing a service to the adult do so in an appropriate way and in a way which values them as individuals. In our case study about Susan in Chapter 2, it would be important that the assessment addressed issues regarding how she communicates through her behaviour and how to support her when she becomes anxious. It could be a lack of information due to a cursory or incomplete assessment, which means that her behaviour is misunderstood and as a result she is not only unsupported but misjudged and even feared. This highlights the role that all workers play in the provision of services which safeguard adults rather than perpetuate misunderstanding and a denial of rights.

An assessment should have the assessed person at the centre of it and should therefore be a participatory process (Milner and O'Byrne, 2002, p. 17) and if this is done, then services should get an accurate picture of what is important to an individual and how they would want to be supported.

The concept of Person Centred Planning (PCP) as advocated in the White Paper *Valuing People* (Department of Health, 2001) has been developed particularly with adults with a learning disability in mind.

PCP aims to emphasise abilities and aspirations rather than the needs emphasis of community care assessments; it attempts to include family and wider social networks as well as statutory resources and emphasises the support necessary to achieve goals (Mansell and Beadle-Brown, 2005, p. 20). Duffy and Sanderson (2005) have commented 'Care managers can fulfil a useful role in co-ordinating services to disabled people and other people who need support. They should work in a spirit of equal exchange and partnership using the techniques of PCP' (p. 48). If assessments are carried out in the spirit of PCP, where a person is seen as central to their assessment and is enabled to express their dreams and aspirations as well as the tasks they need support with, then this sets the context and the tone for a service to be provided which responds to the individual as a whole rather than just as a number of needs or risks which have to be addressed. There are various tools designed to help with PCP (see Part Four) and when the approach is used well, the outcomes for people in terms of living their lives in a way they want to, rather than in a way dictated by services and professionals, has been evidenced. Sanderson *et al.* (2006), refer to the research findings from a report by Robertson in 2005. They state:

> After its [PCP's] introduction, for those who received a plan, positive changes were found in six areas: social networks, contact with family, community activities, and choice. PCP resulted in a 52 per cent increase in the size of social networks, a 140 per cent increase in contact with family, a 40 per cent increase in the level of contact with friends, a 30 per cent increase in the number of community activities, a 33 per cent increase in hours per week of scheduled day activities and 180 per cent more choice. (p. 19)

Although the research claimed that PCP worked better for some people than others (p. 20) the benefits of such an approach are obvious. An approach based on the principles of PCP fits exactly with the philosophy of safeguarding adults by providing them with an environment in which they are enabled to exercise their rights as citizens and are supported in their choices. One of the important lessons from the PCPs of which I have personally been aware is that a lot of the expressed wishes do not have huge cost implications, but are about how someone wants to be supported, referred to, included in decisions and what they like or don't like. In other words, the changes that they would like are often about the everyday things most of us take for granted. They are the kind of changes that are necessary if vulnerable adults are to enjoy the same rights as other citizens; these are the kind of changes that are necessary if services are to be responsive to not only needs, but wishes. In other words, this change in approach to assessment and service provision is necessary if self-determination is to be within the reach of those who are cared for or supported by others.

Care plans

Once an assessment is completed then care planning, which identifies how the assessed needs are to be met, should follow. Again, this is important as the services commissioned should be able to provide an environment which is not abusive in itself but which more positively promotes rights and supports adults appropriately. Agencies then usually write their own care plans once they are offering a service, which outline in more detail how a person should be supported. Many service providers are adopting models of PCP, especially day services' providers. These plans are really important as they should outline to those who support the individuals how to support them in a way which maximises their potential, ensures their rights are not infringed and states the person's preferences. Care plans can have this crucial role, but in order for this to happen, they have to be well thought through, to have at the centre of the process the person themselves and to be used as a tool rather than just be a 'paper exercise'.

Reviews

Reviews should take place at regular intervals, and again, they can have a crucial role in safeguarding adults. A review should have at the centre the individual whose needs are being reviewed. They should look at how needs might have changed and how the service is meeting these needs, since it is possible to have reviews which do not really address any of the important issues for a person and leave them receiving a service which is either abusive or does not value them as an individual. For a review to be effective, by which I mean that it does address such issues, the person conducting the review should have a good idea of what matters to the individual before the meeting. It is very difficult for a lot of people to state what they need in a meeting with professionals and possibly family members present. The review might take the form of a number of meetings or consultations. I would suggest the best way to do this is to meet with the person prior to the meeting or meetings and to agree with them how they would like their views expressed in the meeting.

Some professionals may be tempted to say that a number of adults just cannot be included in an assessment, care plan or review due to their communication or behavioural needs or maybe their cognitive ability, but the challenge is for the professional to find a way in which these people can be included as fully as possible. This may be by observing behaviour and using communication methods other than verbal speech and in the case of those with dementia, it would also include asking relatives or those in a supporting role, what the individual may have wanted in the past. Conducting the processes using whatever means are deemed the most effective way of having the adult's wishes not just heard but central to the process, will help to foster an environment where adults are safeguarded.

There are challenges on how to carry out these principles in practice. What is important is the attitude of people who support adults in various ways. Workers should have at the centre of their thinking not only the rights of those they support but also the role they have in supporting them in these rights. It is also important that workers look at their own work practices and those of others to see what impact they are having on the lives of others. A healthy culture in which services are offered is one where debate takes place between workers on the support they offer and where people are not afraid to re-examine routines, practices, long held ideas and the 'way things are'. This takes courage, both personal and professional, and may be met with resistance from some who have a closed mind or who, for whatever reason, find change threatening to them personally.

Direct Payments

The development of Direct Payments so that an individual can purchase their own care and be the employers of their carers rather than a recipient of a service is to be applauded. The White Paper *Our Health, Our Care, Our Say: A New Direction for Community Services* was launched in January 2006 (DoH, 2006) . It places an increased emphasis on individual budgets with the aim that people will be given greater choice and realise a greater degree of independence. Greater choice for people is obviously an aim which is laudable. However, with increased opportunities come increased risks. It is important that those who are employed to provide support are not only competent, but do so in such a way that people are safe from any form of abuse and are respected as individuals. The role of being an employer does give the adult power, but they can still be victim to inappropriate or abusive 'care' and may feel reluctant or unable to address issues or to dismiss a person when they can be taken to an industrial tribunal if a claim of unfair dismissal is made.

Individualised budgets are a very new idea at the time of writing and not widely understood. Under this system, people will be told what resources are available to meet their needs, together with the cost of these services. Duffy (2006) explains the significance of such a system:

> What may lead to powerful changes is a combining of this knowledge with rules and systems that enable the person to decide how the available funding will be used. This alternative system for organising social care is called self-directed support. In fact it is only really possible to make good sense of the idea of an individual budget in the context of self-directed support. Knowledge of the resources available, on its own and without the power to control them, will only lead to frustration. The knowledge must be functional for the individual in order to be meaningful. (p. 4)

If such a new system is to be successfully implemented, then the way services are used will change. Duffy talks of a 'transfer of power' (p. 9) and comments that 'many existing systems, policies and structures will need to support the culture of self-directed support'. The shape of community care may be changing and there may be more power given to adults to take some responsibility for managing their own individual system of support. The principles I have outlined will remain exactly the same, even in this radically different way in which services will be commissioned. The fact that more power will be given to adults will be a very positive move, but it must be seen in the context of a society which will still marginalise certain groups.

There are some real dangers as well as huge benefits from such a new system. Families might play a larger part in deciding who should provide support as they will not necessarily be just tapping into existing services. Again, this could be extremely positive except in those families where the adult is already experiencing abuse or being subjected to inappropriate care. I am not advocating that 'professional' support is always the best outcome or that people are not to be trusted with managing their own care. Any system where adults are able to choose how and by whom they are supported is a much better system than has been the case where they are largely fitted into already existing services. The danger is that adults could exercise this choice and yet still find that they are not supported in the way they want to be or offered appropriate respect or kept safe from harm. The challenge for support providers to think through how they work with and support an adult will be every bit as pertinent as it is now.

Points to ponder

This chapter has covered quite a lot of ground in examining guidance documents and looking at legal interventions. The following is a list of questions which I hope you will find useful to consider for your role in safeguarding adults:

➤ What does your agency policy say you should do if you become aware of a potential situation of adult abuse? What should you record and who should you report it to?

➤ Do you feel confident enough to follow the practice guidelines if an adult discloses abuse to you? This obviously presupposes that you are familiar with them. If you do not feel confident enough, you should discuss this with your manager and they should support you in accessing appropriate training.

➤ Are you clear about how your attitudes and actions resulting from these attitudes can restrict a person's independence and infringe their rights?

➤ If you work in a hospital where people are detained, do you think all the procedures and practices are beneficial to the adults or do any hinder their recovery and oppress rather than support them?

Chapter 4

Issues in Relation to Family Carers

I have been concerned about the rights of the people you work with so far and this is an appropriate emphasis and fundamental principle which should underpin all practice. However, there can be situations where it is difficult to balance the rights of an adult with the rights of a family member who is caring for them. Carers are very much on the government agenda as playing a role in the provision of support to adults. Carers have a right to an assessment in their own right, regardless of whether or not the person they are caring for wants one. Under the Carers (Equal Opportunities) Act 2004 the local authority has to consider their wishes to work, as well as whether they are undertaking or wish to undertake education, training or a leisure activity.

There is growing awareness of the needs of unpaid or family carers as well as the important role they play. A balance has to found in an attitude towards carers as it is easy to take a polarised and ultimately unhelpful view. On the one hand it is possible to adopt a negative attitude which views the way they support or care for someone with suspicion. On the other hand it is possible to work with the carers in a way that can exclude the adult who is being supported, as the professional can be pulled into colluding against the very person they are working with. The way to avoid falling into either of these two positions is to have an awareness of the difficulties which unpaid carers face, but at the same time be able to discern when the difficulties are leading to an abusive experience for the person being cared for. The stresses placed on carers by unrelenting and prolonged periods of caring for someone can be seen as a cause of conditions which decline into abusive situations. It is important to stress that this is only part of the picture of why adults are abused, but it is an important part to recognise.

Role of a carer

The role of a carer is a complex one as is the relationship they have with the person being cared for. In this chapter I will be referring to unpaid or family carers, those people who offer care and support to an adult, usually as a result of an already existing relationship. Taylor and Dodd (2003) (quoted in Manthorpe *et al.*, 2005), carried out a study of staff attitudes towards adult protection of people working in health, social services and other statutory agencies. They found that only 41 per cent of their respondents stated that sexual partners could abuse and only half identified neglect as a form of abuse. This is interesting as it demonstrates a number of issues; firstly, 59 per cent of respondents thought that partners either don't or can't abuse those they care for and secondly, that neglect is not seen as a form of abuse.

Attitudes towards family carers vary between workers as can be seen from Taylor and Dodd's study. It is important that we get the balance right. A view that is wholly suspicious of carers is unhelpful at best and generally oppressive. On the other hand, a view which sees carers as above suspicion and as some kind of special or saintly person is also unhelpful and can be oppressive towards those they care for as they are viewed as a 'burden'. It is also oppressive towards the carers as this attitude can lead to needs being unrecognised and certainly unacknowledged.

With the arrival of legislation that obligates statutory agencies to offer assessments to carers in their own right (Carers and Disabled Children Act 2000 and Carers (Equal Opportunities) Act 2004) comes a new emphasis on the needs of carers. It is important that the needs of both the 'cared for' and those doing the caring are balanced and that any stresses on the carer are recognised in a way that does not stigmatise either them or the person they are caring for. There is a real need for workers to hold a balanced view of carers and not to make any assumptions. While family carers are to be valued and supported it is important to be aware that a lot of abuse does occur in family settings. The Government's response to the recommendations and conclusions of the Health Select Committee's Inquiry into Elder Abuse (DoH, 2004) states:

> Abuse in domiciliary settings is the commonest type of abuse, but the most difficult to combat. Contact between victims of abuse and statutory services may be limited, and those abused will often feel under threat, or obligation, to those abusing them. The only measures likely to have much impact here would be ones which increased the climate of awareness of the problem, making health and social care professionals more aware of the issue, and those which empowered older people to report abuse more easily, recognising the reasons for their reluctance to do so. (p. 3)

The report recommends awareness training for those professionals who come into contact with older people living at home as well as the use of advocates, but it acknowledges that this is a 'difficult problem . . . with no simple solutions' (p. 3). The issues are not unique to older people, but are equally pertinent to any adult who is 'cared for' in their family home, including, for example, adults with a learning or physical impairment or mental health needs.

Carers and structural oppression

It is important that carers are seen within the context of structural oppression, just as those they care for should be. Caring is a low status role in society and it suits the economic priorities of society that adults are cared for within their families as this is the cheapest way of providing care. Direct Payments are only allowed to be used to pay for care from a family member living with the person being cared for under exceptional circumstances. The assumption is that care provided by family members who live with the person should be provided at no cost to the state, apart from certain welfare benefits received, but this is not the same as receiving a wage. Webb and Tossell (1999) identify the situation of carers within society. Referring to the image projected by the media and official organisations of society they state:

> The image projected is often one of a stable, balanced society that rewards best those who are talented or hard-working, and ascribes failure either to individual pathology or to misfortune. In other words, the individual is considered to be responsible for his or her circumstances. It is rarely admitted that hardship is structurally determined. (p. 223)

The challenge to workers is to understand that carers experience hardship, but this is structurally determined. In other words, society expects that a family will look after one of their own members, and that if this is not done, there is a certain amount of blame attached to that, especially to female family members, as women in particular are expected to provide a caring role. Stereotypical assumptions may be made in relation to a black older person as this quotation from *Social Work Today* illustrates;

> There is a racist-orientated myth that should be written on the tombstone of every black, elderly person who dies, alone and poor, unaware of the services which could have advanced their later years – they look after their own. (*Social Work Today*, 24 March 1988, p. 28, quoted in Webb and Tossell, 1999, p. 109)

'Hardship'

The 'hardship' endured by carers might be financial, in terms of relying on benefits or having to juggle part-time jobs with caring; psychological, as the stress of constantly caring can be emotionally draining; or physical, as the task may involve heavy lifting of someone who needs support to move. It could be that the carer is on the receiving end of violent actions from the person they are supporting. You must be vigilant not to fall into the trap of assuming that the carer has to be some sort of martyr, or that they are responsible for the situation they find themselves in. The role of the carer should be viewed within the framework of structural oppression and that those who provide care for family members do what society expects them to do.

It is important to respect the rights of the adults being supported as I have stated throughout this book, but at the same time recognise the implications that supporting them at home might have on a family member. Viewing them both within the structural context not only provides a broader context in which to understand the position of the adult being cared for and their carer, but also identifies both parties as belonging to groups that are marginalised by society.

This is not to say that any abuse by carers is to be overlooked, but that their role is seen in context and that they are performing the role that society expects of them.

One difficulty I have found is how to balance on the one hand the belief in the right of citizenship for adults being cared for and on the other hand to acknowledge that this is sometimes at a high personal cost to those caring for them. To understand their joint situation in this light helps with that dilemma. They are both oppressed at the structural level of Thompson's analysis (see Part Three of this book), and they are marginalised from work, as it is very difficult to work full-time and provide a caring role.

Buckner and Yeandle (2006) in their paper for Carers UK *What Carers Need*, quote statistics from the 2001 Census and draw the following conclusions:

1. Men and women are more likely to be employed part-time rather than full-time when they are carers.
2. More of them look after their home and family on a full-time basis.

Political context of caring

Carers, then, are statistically more likely to be either unemployed or working part-time, and the financial implication of this is obvious. This has a triple disadvantage as not only are they financially disadvantaged because their caring role is not remunerated, but they are excluded from full-time employment, which in a capitalist society is highly valued. Also, instead of being employed they take part in work which is not valued by society as it is not 'productive'. To understand that this is the political context of caring is not to view the caring role as inferior to any other role or to view it as a 'tragedy' for both the carer and the adult who needs support. Instead, it is to recognise that some people do have needs which mean that without support they would not achieve any form of independence. It also means recognising that society expects some people, because of their gender or even race, to fulfil that role.

Of course many carers take on the role willingly, but that does not mean that they are any less subjected to this form of social control as they have been socialised into believing that they should take on the role. They might still willingly take on the role, even if they did have an appreciation of this pressure, but for them to understand this might make these people less reluctant to accept support for themselves as they believe they are failing in some way if they cannot cope.

Watson (2006) has written a paper for Carers UK examining the rights of carers in relation to the Human Rights Act 1998 and points out a number of areas where the Act is being breached. Article 2 states that people have the right to have their own life protected by law. Carers do not always take due regard to their own health as they can put the needs of the person they are supporting before their own. Article 3 states that people have a right to be free from inhuman or degrading treatment. Watson maintains that carers can suffer from acute mental health problems as a result of their caring role. Article 8 states that people have the right to respect of their privacy and family life. Watson explains how carers find it difficult to achieve a balance between their own rights and the person they are caring for as she maintains that social services departments tell them they may not get the services they need even if they get an assessment.

Complexity of working with carers

If it is part of your role to work with family carers, it can appear daunting as you may think you have no hope on your own of addressing the complexity of the issues. You may feel this way as the situation of family carers is due, at least in part, to the way society is structured. However, as will be discussed in Part Three, although individual workers have the most influence at the personal level, that does not mean they do not have any influence at the cultural and structural levels. The way carers are worked with, included in an appropriate way, and allowed to have a voice, will have an impact on the cultural and structural levels, even if this is on a small scale.

The reason I have been looking at the role of carers is that as already stated, it has been observed that most adult abuse takes place within the home. The government has stressed the importance of carers in *Caring for Carers* (DoH, 1999a) and in the foreword, Prime Minister Tony Blair, stated; 'In communities, the networks of giving, of caring, and of supporting relatives, friends and neighbours are part of the glue that helps join society together' (p. 11). Although a distinct moral tone is discernable in the statement, it does highlight the dilemma for workers in working with carers. On the one hand, they provide the 'glue' that joins society together while on the other, it is at the hand of carers that adults are most likely to experience abuse. How can these two such opposite positions or views of carers be reconciled?

I want to consider two case studies at this point to demonstrate the type of circumstances in which a carer might be offering care or support to someone living with them.

Case study 1

Betty and Bernard have been married for 45 years. Bernard has dementia and Betty has been supporting him at home. They had a loving relationship before Bernard's dementia, but Bernard tended to make all the major decisions about their lives. They have three grown-up children, who all live at least 40 miles away and work full-time. Betty used to like to visit friends and although she spent a lot of time with Bernard as well, her friendships were an important part of her life. Recently, she has felt unable to leave Bernard so she has stopped visiting her friends. Her friends used to come to see her, but Betty has stopped inviting them as Bernard's behaviour has become unpredictable and he has embarrassed both Betty and her friends by his comments to them. Betty used to be able to rest at night, but lately Bernard seems to have lost all sense of time and will often get up in the middle of the night, get dressed and try and leave the house as he will be convinced that he has an appointment to which he must get, or he will start turning on the appliances in the kitchen. Betty is really worried about her own and Bernard's safety, but feels she cannot keep an eye on him all of the time as she is getting more and more tired. She has been feeling increasingly depressed and has several times just stopped herself from striking out at Bernard when he has been up in the middle of the night putting on all the appliances. Betty feels that she does not want to tell their children how things really are as they think she is coping so well.

Case study 2

Chakor has been caring for his brother Shamas for ten years, ever since their mother died. Shamas has Autism and can get very upset if his routine is varied or if anything unpredictable happens. Shamas has one CD which he plays over and over again very loudly and gets very upset if Chakor asks him to turn it down or not to listen to it. Shamas cannot tolerate using glass or china and if he sees anything that is made out of either, he tries to smash it. Shamas has a fascination with water and sometimes gets up in the middle of the night, puts all of his clothes in the bath and turns the taps on. This has caused flooding a few times and of course means that Shamas has no dry clothes to wear in the morning. Shamas seems to like living with Chakor and Chakor is certainly very patient with him and he does his best to meet his brother's needs. Chakor is working full-time, while his brother is at college and in the evenings he is busy with all tasks involved in caring for his brother. Chakor would like to pursue a relationship of his own and have his own family, but he feels that he has an obligation to his brother as he promised their mother that he would 'take care of him'.

The case studies are about situations that have changed and brought with them dramatic changes to the lives of the two carers. In the first study, mental illness has changed the relationship of Bernard and Betty. What was once a mutually supportive relationship has become one in which Betty is providing all the support for Bernard and instead of Bernard being her lifetime confidante and best friend, he has become someone who no longer knows who she is all the time and whose behaviour presents a risk to the safety of them both. In the second case study, the death of Chakor's and Shamas' mother meant that Chakor felt he should continue to provide the support which had been provided by their mother. Chakor's life has been restricted and as tied to routine as his brother's is.

Both case studies are based on elements taken from actual situations and do reflect the kind of complex issues which typify the relationship between carers and those they care for or support. They certainly do not exaggerate the kind of situations in which carers find themselves. The needs of both the carer and the cared for should be recognised and addressed. It would not be surprising if either Betty or Chakor became exhausted both emotionally and physically. They are already both socially isolated, although Chakor does work. It does not take much of a leap of imagination to see that Betty and Chakor could act in a way they would not normally do if they did not have support in terms of their own needs. Betty could find herself in a position where she strikes out at Bernard through sheer exhaustion and frustration at the changes that have taken place in him and, as a consequence, in her life. Chakor could become so tired and worn down by the continual playing of the same CD and the continual vigilance with the water that he could lose his temper and strike out or shout at Shamas.

In these circumstances, it is important to recognise that everyone has limited resources in terms of energy, time and patience and with the best will in the world, everyone has a point at which they will act in a way they wouldn't otherwise.

Situations such as these can be supported in a number of ways and the carers can be given a break from their duties. One way in which this has been achieved is through what was called 'respite care', but now is increasingly being called 'short breaks'. This change in language is a recognition that the term 'respite' care was not a positive one as it implied the need for a period of 'respite' from the person being cared for. This tended to produce a negative image of the adult being cared for rather than the term 'short break', which is much more neutral. The break should be viewed both as a break from the person caring as well as for the person caring. In other words, it should be mutually beneficial. Traditionally, this has taken the form of the person being cared for going to stay at a unit for short breaks or with a family who are approved by the local authority. There are other models for this and someone with Shamas' needs may benefit from someone coming to care for or support him in his own home while Chakor pursues his own interests. Whatever is provided to support carers like Betty and Chakor, will minimise the likelihood of them becoming so exhausted that they end up abusing the very person they are caring for.

When carers have complex needs

There are other situations where the carer has their own needs which impair their ability to provide appropriate care. There seems to have been an example of this in the case of Beverley Lewis, already cited. In this case her mother had mental health needs and a failure to address the needs of the two women separately seems to have been a contributory factor in Beverley's death. It is vital that situations such as these, where the carer has their own needs which could impair their ability to care, are considered carefully. On the one hand, it would be oppressive practice and discriminatory to assume that someone with a learning or physical impairment could not care adequately for another person. On the other hand, however, it is extremely poor practice to assume that all will be well and to shy away from considering the person's ability to care because the professional is frightened of being discriminatory. The way to practice in an appropriate way is not to make assumptions, but to judge each situation individually. If there are concerns about how someone is being cared for or supported, then it is the responsibility of the professional to either address these themselves, or to pass on these concerns, depending on their role.

When carers abuse

There are other situations where an adult is being wilfully and maliciously abused by family or other informal carers. These situations require that action is taken through the criminal justice system. These are situations where older people, learning disabled, physically impaired adults or those with mental ill-health are subjected to acts which are intended to hurt them either physically, emotionally, psychologically or financially.

As I have already stated earlier, these situations are the very ones which may not be investigated as they are the situations where the adult may not have access to other people, and if they do, they may be too frightened to say what is happening to them. This highlights the vital importance of acting if you do ever have any cause to believe that someone is being abused. If you do not act, then maybe no one else will either. We all have the duty to report what we suspect as citizens and that duty seems to me all the more compelling if these concerns are raised during the course of our work.

Risk factors for older people being abused

Kurrle (2001) identified risk factors for older people in terms of the likelihood of them being abused. She states:

> Research and clinical experiences show very clearly that there are a number of factors contributing to the occurrence of abuse and a combination of these are usually involved in abusive situations. (p. 97)

She cites five risk factors:

1. Increased dependency of the older person as they are dependent on others for assistance.
2. Abuser psychopathology as the personality characteristics of the abuser are significant in the likelihood of them abusing. A carer who is an alcoholic, a drug addict or has a mental impairment or a mental health need is seen as having

characteristics which are 'highly significant as contributory factors in cases of abuse'.
3. Family dynamics, as domestic violence is considered as being 'normal' in some families. Other factors could be that the person caring for was once abused by the person they are supporting or marital conflict can continue into old age and become abuse.
4. Carer stress, as lack of support, illness, financial worries or personal worries can all lead to stress.
5. Older population, as with the increase of demands on community resources which are not always readily available then it seems as if there will be a growing reliance on carers. With an ageing population and with it an increase in dementia and other illnesses, it seems as if there will be a growing strain placed on them. (p. 97-8)

Although Kurrle was analysing the situation in Australia and only in relation to older people, her work provides a useful analysis for the UK. I would though, urge caution in the application of these risk factors as they are useful in highlighting the likelihood of abuse, but that does not mean that it will or must occur. There may also be situations which do not fit into any of the risk factors, but are clearly abusive. Care must also be taken in the use of Kurrle's second risk factor as assumptions must not be made by anyone working with carers that because they have certain characteristics, then they will abuse or be unable to offer appropriate care and support. It is useful to know that there may be an increased risk of carers with identified characteristics providing unsafe care or being perpetrators of abuse, but to make an assumption that this is the case is oppressive and discriminatory. The identification of carers' stress resulting from lack of support, illness, financial worries or their own personal worries seem to be the same issues as are reported in the UK.

Young carers

There is growing awareness of the role of young carers offering care and support to family members. Young carers have been defined as 'a child or young person (under age 18) who is carrying out significant caring tasks and assuming a level of responsibility for another (adult) person, which would normally be taken by an adult' (DoH, 1997, p. 1). Young carers may provide support with a range of needs including personal care as well as domestic chores and paperwork. They may also play a role in looking after siblings and in providing emotional support. A young carer may provide appropriate support and it is important that assumptions are not made about them or the quality of care they provide. The view that young carers are 'robbed of their childhood' is to be challenged as it presupposes that young people should not have a role in supporting their family members. The other extreme view, that it is their role to be a carer out of a sense of family duty, is also to be challenged as this is equally oppressive. A balanced view is needed where young carers are free to carry out the tasks they are happy to do, but not to the detriment of their own education or social and emotional development.

Our Health, Our Care, Our Say: A New Direction for Community Services

The White Paper *Our Health, Our Care, Our Say: A New Direction for Community Services*, (DoH, 2006) launched in January 2006, confirms the government agenda in increasing the importance placed on the role of carers. Some of the proposed changes (at the time of writing) are:

- A new information service/helpline for carers, which may be run by a voluntary organisation.
- Short breaks to be established in every council area.
- An expert carers programme to provide training for carers will be established.

These are all developments to be welcomed as, if implemented fully, they will meet some of the needs expressed by carers. However, they will only be useful if they completely address carers' needs and not just equip them to better provide a free service. It is, of course, really important that carers receive support, advice and training in their role, but this is to be seen in the context of a society where they are at the same time expected to perform the caring role and are marginalised for doing so. In terms of providing an environment in which adults are 'safeguarded', which is the expressed aim of the *Safeguarding Adults* document, these are all laudable aims. It seems sensible that if carers are provided with training and support, then they will be better equipped to offer an environment in which the adult they are caring for is safeguarded and the likelihood of unsafe care or abuse being perpetrated is minimised. It will be interesting to see what impact these proposals make once they have been implemented.

The reason I have spent quite a lot of time looking at issues for carers is, as already stated, the fact that most abuse is experienced in people's own homes. As I have shown, there have been various explanations offered as to why this might be the case. A balanced view has been emphasised as being necessary for workers. A view is needed in which we recognise the marginalisation of carers by society; see their needs as individuals and in relation to their ability to continue to offer care and support. We must also recognise that there are risks associated with adults being cared for at home in terms of abuse issues. It is equally important that the person being supported is viewed as a person with their own rights and needs and not as a 'burden' on either the carer or society.

Points to ponder

It might be helpful for you to think of the following questions for your own personal reflection but also as points for discussion with others:

> How do you think of family carers? Do you regard them in a positive light or a negative one?
> Do you feel sorry for carers as they seem to have an exhausting task? If you do, who or what do you blame for this?
> If you had reason to suspect a carer with whom you had a good relationship was abusing the person they cared for, what would you do? What should you do (in line with policies and procedures)?

Chapter 5
Service User Involvement

The relevance of this chapter may not be immediately obvious, although service user involvement is highly relevant to our consideration of safeguarding adults. Firstly, it is relevant in terms of providing a service which is responsive to individuals and enables adults to live as independently as possible. When people are involved in planning and reviewing the services they use, then we have the opportunity to be responsive to the comments of those who know what it is like to be a service user and also know how services can be improved.

Secondly, it is relevant in relation to adult protection issues so adults can have a say in interventions which may be prompted as a result of concerns for their safety. Service user involvement is important as it is another way of supporting adults in their rights as citizens.

Service user involvement and participation

Throughout the book I have been considering issues of best practice in terms of working with the adults we support or care for. 'Service user involvement' is considered crucial to this and is certainly 'fashionable thinking' at the moment. The danger with fashionable thinking is that people talk about it because they know it is regarded as important, but may not accept the principles at any deep or meaningful level so lip service only is paid.

Thompson (1998) stresses the importance of 'participation' and sees it as a 'practice principle'. He asserts that it 'can be seen as a broader form of partnership in which collaboration occurs not only at micro-level of specific practice situations, but also at the wider levels of service planning; policy development and evaluation; training' (p. 213). The implication of this is that service user participation plays a really important role in the different levels of Thompson's PCS analysis (see Part Three for discussion of analysis). At the personal level it is important that adults are able to be involved and consulted in decisions about themselves and have a say in how they are cared for, supported and spoken to. At the cultural level, if adults are consulted more, this will become 'how things are done' instead of much current practice where they have to fit into and conform to the way things are in the organisations from which they receive support. At the structural level, if adults who use services are consulted in terms of policies and service planning, then policies and plans will become less oppressive. Also, if service users are involved in training, then this will help to influence and promote change at all levels by making workers more aware of the viewpoints of the adults they support and understand their experiences more. This in turn should influence the thinking and behaviour of workers in the way they support people, include them in decisions and develop services and policies.

Participation, then, has two important and distinct roles in our consideration of safeguarding adults. Firstly, it has a role in that adults should be not only involved in but central to decisions that are made about them, and as has been stated throughout the book this includes issues in relation to adult protection. Secondly, it has a role in how all services are developed. This is a really important part of safeguarding adults as we can only really hope to provide services that ensure an environment which maximises independence and is free from abuse and poor practice, if we know what is acceptable to those who receive such services. This is not to say that professionals do not have any understanding of the needs of people, but that this understanding needs to be 'grounded' in what people say about their experiences of receiving those services.

The involvement of adults directly in their own abuse investigation can raise practice issues when, for example, an adult lacks capacity. Although the principle is straightforward, the application may be far from that. Banks (2006) questions what terms like 'participation' and 'involvement' mean as they can be used rather loosely:

> While the consultation and involvement of service users should no doubt be a right, 'participation' in the strong sense of joint or full decision making powers will usually depend on the capacity of the service user to make the decision. (p. 118)

Banks provides us with a useful framework for considering involvement and participation in terms of safeguarding adults. If consultation and involvement are rights, then it is important to ensure that adults are consulted and involved. I have already looked at how people should be included in assessments, care plans and reviews as well as specific processes in terms of adult protection such as attendance at, and involvement in, a case conference. This principle should be applied and adults should be consulted in such a way that they are able to understand fully what is being discussed or decided upon. Participation, as Banks has intimated, will depend on the capacity of the individual. Participation is, however, to be aimed at in every case, but this might be achieved in different ways.

Sometimes situations arise where, for various reasons, unfounded allegations are made by service users. If a person has a history of making unfounded allegations, then good practice dictates that each allegation should still be taken seriously. Work may be needed to help the individual understand the consequences of making false allegations and the effect this has on other people. The fact that a false allegation has been made once does not mean that future allegations will also be false and these will still require investigation. The danger here is that allegations may not be reported at all. Adults who make false allegations do present challenges to the people who support them, but they must still be safeguarded. In the context of participation, how to support such a person to participate may be a challenge, but this must still be considered. It may even be the case that participation and actually seeing the consequences of the allegation in terms of the investigation may be a deterrent for further false allegations.

The role of advocates

The use of an independent advocate can be an effective way of enabling someone to participate. Independent advocates are used a lot in work with adults with a learning disability or mental health needs. They can have a number of roles, all of which can support a more participatory process. Advocates can:

- Speak on behalf of someone else when they find it difficult to speak for themselves.
- Support someone in speaking up for themselves.
- Get to know someone who is unable to speak up for themselves and try and speak on their behalf in the way the advocate believes they would if they were able to.

Advocates are independent in that they do not work for statutory agencies and so are not constrained in the same way as a professional within one would be. They can play a crucial role in supporting or speaking on behalf of an adult, with part of their role being to put themselves 'in the shoes' of the person they are advocating for. This sounds straightforward but can be problematic as advocates, just like everyone else, have their own personal values and could inflict these (knowingly or otherwise) on the person they are advocating for. Having said that they can play a very important role and certainly help address the question of how participation can be achieved for someone unable to speak for themselves. It is vital that people who are unable to speak up for themselves do have independent representation as although social workers or other professionals may seek to represent the person as well as they can, they are also agents of their own agency and ultimately of the state and so this can be problematic. Consider the following case study.

Case study

John has a severe learning disability and does not communicate verbally. He gets distressed when he is spoken to for very long and when someone says more than a few words to him, he will get very anxious and begin to vocalise loudly and then to bite his hand if they persist. John lives in a group home where it was thought he was being neglected. An investigation has been completed although the findings were inconclusive. CSCI have recommended that the group home put in place some improvements, including training for staff members and they will monitor the implementation of them, but they do not think the situation is serious enough to close the home. John has a sister who has always been pleased that John is living in the group home, as she feels he is safe and well cared for there. She will not contemplate the idea of John moving. John was referred to an Advocacy service as his social worker thought that his own 'voice' could get lost as his sister and staff at the home have strong feelings about him staying there.

In the case study, it is difficult to determine directly what John wants. Although the home was not closed and recommendations were implemented, his social worker thought that he might benefit from a move. The role of an advocate for John would be to give him a 'voice' in any decisions that are made and to address the balance of power that staff and his sister have in that they are able to speak very forcibly about what they think is best for John. The advocate should get to know John, find out what is important to him and what he finds stressful, as well as what he likes. The advocate should not be influenced by John's social worker's negative opinion of the home, but by what is important to John. This is obviously a very skilled role for an advocate but when the role is carried out correctly, it will ensure at least that John does have a voice and that this situation is not just a battle of the wills between two opposing parties.

Participation in service development

As we have seen, the first form of service user participation I have identified is when they are involved in their own abuse or safeguarding investigation. The second form of participation with adults who receive services is when they are consulted (and listened to) in relation to how the services are developed. This can take many forms; from consulting with existing groups, asking individuals to comment on their experiences, seeking feedback from all who use services, commissioning independent research into people's experiences and views, to including service users in planning and policy making forums.

All of these methods could be just another way of oppressing rather than including people, if they are not thought through properly. Issues such as appropriate ways of communicating, how to make individuals feel comfortable, when is the best time to include them, where consultation takes place and whether views are representative, rather than just the issues of one particular person, all need to be considered. If these issues are not addressed, then poor practice can be duplicated and the opportunity to learn from people lost. An example of this would be if an adult with mental health needs is asked to comment on the flexibility of services to her needs at a time when she is particularly low in mood and unable to respond as she could at other times. Not only has the person who is seeking her views not found out what they are, but by failing to find out what her needs might be, has replicated the poor practice they are seeking to address in others. I am sure you can think of similar examples which are relevant to the adults you work with. It is of course, vital that issues of race and culture are considered or the consultation process will just replicate the discrimination experienced in services.

Services which provide residential accommodation to people can develop forums in which adults can express their views. It is important to address issues of power in any such forum as a member of staff chairing or even just attending can prevent people expressing their views. An advocate might have a useful role in such a meeting by supporting someone in feeding back to staff what their concerns are. Such changes can be somewhat difficult to implement as they may be very different from what people have experienced and resistance may be expressed. The reason that such changes can be resisted is that they upset the balance of power, but this is of course the object of the exercise. Even if workers are not conscious of the power they do have, they will try and maintain it.

However service users are involved, the important thing is that they are, and in a way that it not just tokenistic but does initiate change.

Points to ponder

Consider the following questions in relation to your own agency and your own practice:

➤ How do you consult with the adults you support about your own practice?
➤ How do you ensure the adults you support are involved in decisions that are made about them?
➤ What are your agency policies about service user participation?
➤ What role do service users have in the formation of policies and the development of policies in your agency?

Part Three: Discrimination and Oppression

Chapter 6
What has Safeguarding Adults to do with Discrimination and Oppression?

This part of the book is concerned with ways in which theory addresses discrimination and oppression. I will use Thompson's PCS analysis to identify ways in which discrimination is perpetuated. As our concern is with safeguarding adults, I will particularly look at the role of the family and workplace culture in the creation and continuation of either good or poor ways of working with adults. I will also briefly examine the role that values play in the way we support individuals. I have included a discussion of religious beliefs as I believe this provides a good example of when personal beliefs and professional values can be at odds with each other.

Thompson's PCS analysis

I have discussed already the definition of a 'vulnerable adult' and seen that it can infer a deficit model that leaves the vulnerability with the adult, rather than leaving the 'victimising' with the individual or group of individuals who mistreat the adult in some way. It is helpful to concentrate on the people or systems who victimise the adults as this can help us to understand how this happens. Thompson's PCS analysis is often used to gain an understanding of how individuals are oppressed or victimised. In this model, three levels are highlighted within which people are situated and experience oppression. The three levels, personal (*P*), cultural (*C*) and structural (*S*) operate separately but are also interrelated.

Personal level – P

At the personal level individuals have thoughts, feelings and prejudices which influence how they act towards others. Prejudice is often held without a person really thinking they hold such beliefs as people are brought up with attitudes about others which become deep-seated beliefs. An example of prejudice might be the assumption that older people are not as intelligent as younger ones and become childlike. Such a belief will directly influence the way someone talks to and supports an older person. They may tend to talk 'down' to them, talk slowly and very deliberately and generally talk in a patronising way. They may also make assumptions about their ability to form relationships, or if formed, may assume they are platonic.

I have already looked at numerous practice issues from the personal level throughout this book. Thompson (1998) has cautioned against an over-emphasis of the personal level:

> Although it cannot be denied that prejudiced attitudes and behaviours do exist, we have to be careful to avoid the mistake of attaching too much significance to the personal level. Individual behaviour needs to be understood in its broader context if we are to have more than a partial and distorted view of the situation. The *P* level of prejudice and individual attitudes and actions is only one part of the overall picture. (p. 12)

Part of the personal level is formed by attitudes which are individual to you and which you have developed as part of your biography. You may have had some experience which means that you have a negative view of a specific group of people which is over and above the prejudice that is perpetuated through culture. I know someone who was subject to a racist attack and this compounded the prejudice that he already had for that racial group. It is not logical that just because someone has a negative experience with a few people, that they should regard the entire group to which they are thought to belong in a negative way, but this is what happens. It is a useful exercise to see if there are any instances in your own history which mean that you have difficulty in viewing certain groups of people in a negative way, as only when we analyse our own responses can we begin to address what this means for our own practice.

Cultural level – C

In the PCS analysis, the personal level is embedded in the cultural level. The cultural level refers to the way people live in a particular social group. It includes language and humour, values, accepted practices and behaviours and even the way people dress. Each of us is the product, to a greater or lesser extent, of the culture in which we are immersed. It is very difficult for us to identify our cultural patterns and behaviours as we do not think about these at a conscious level, we just experience them as 'the way things are' and reinforce them by our own acceptance of them and, in continuing to practice them, thus maintain them. Hofstede (1997) refers to culture as 'mental programming' and 'mental software' (p. 4), emphasising the idea that culture sets the framework in which we think. He states:

> Culture . . . is always a collective phenomenon, because it is at least partly shared with people who live or lived within the same social environment, which is where it is learned. It is *the collective programming of the mind which distinguishes the members of one group or category of people from another.*

Culture is learned, not inherited. It derives from one's social environment, not from one's genes. (p. 5)

To apply Hofstede's analogy to the PCS model, the individual programming of the mind is what happens at the *P* level, whereas, 'collective programming' happens and reinforces individual programming at the *C* level.

I am interested in two different cultures here; one is the culture in which we live as individuals and the other is the culture of our workplaces. Thompson's PCS analysis has usually been taken to refer mainly to the former, but it should also be used as an analytical tool for workplace culture and I will now consider this.

Both types of culture are where 'collective programming' takes place and it is important to consider the role of each in the way people think and behave.

Language is particularly significant as it is a real clue to the values of a particular culture. How groups of people are referred to indicates how they are regarded. If one particular group of people is the subject of humour in a disparaging way then it is fairly safe to assume that they are not valued and are being demonised, belittled or dismissed in some way. Humour can seem harmless, but it is a really powerful way in which stereotypes and prejudices are reinforced. It may be that a worker knows it is unacceptable to refer to people in demeaning ways or tell demeaning jokes about the group they work with and so refrain from doing this in the workplace. Just because attitudes are not expressed does not mean they are not present, it just means that a person is able to adapt their behaviour to different settings and behave in ways which they know will be accepted in each. These negative attitudes may not be as evident as when the worker is with friends and is telling jokes which belittle others, but they will influence the way they shape the workplace culture.

There may well be a workplace culture in which workers do belittle others, tell jokes about the people they support or laugh at their mistakes. If this is the case, it is obviously unacceptable, but it is more likely that the culture will have more subtle means of reinforcing negative values. Sometimes, humour can be part of a workplace culture that helps the workers deal with stressful situations. Thought needs to be given in such situations about this use of humour. If it stigmatises the individuals that are being supported, then it is not acceptable. If however, it helps take the stress out of a difficult situation then it may have a useful role to play. This point would make an interesting discussion in a team meeting. I would suggest that the key question might be in relation to what is being laughed at or satirised. If it is the service user, then again, this is not acceptable. If it is a situation, then it might be acceptable. Thinking through the use of humour in your workplace will help you to identify how and why it is being used and decide on its appropriateness or otherwise.

Another example of inappropriateness would be through work practices which do not have the adult being supported at the centre. It is possible to have a workplace culture which is really for the benefit of the workers rather than those who are being supported. An example of this might be where trips out or even holidays are arranged around where staff would like to go rather than around the interests or needs of the adults being supported. This might not look on the surface to be poor practice as people might be included in community activities, but the issue is that it is all about staff and what they want to do. This is just as demeaning to the adults but in a much more subtle way. The value is still the same, namely that this group of people is not valued as highly as others, but the cultural expression of it is different. I would not want to suggest that it is inappropriate for people to support others to enjoy the activities, but it is a matter of why things are done and for whose benefit. Values can be carefully disguised and packaged to look like good practice when they are in fact the cultural expression of prejudice.

Thompson (1998) explains the importance of culture in our understanding of discrimination and oppression. It has a role as a 'boundary marker', and serves to exclude other groups, the creation of the 'us and them' situations. It can also be a vehicle for racism as that is partly based on the assumption of cultural superiority (p. 15). These points can also be applied to workplace culture. There is obviously a clear distinction between those paid to support or work with someone and those who receive the support or service. To suggest otherwise would be to make the same error as people who do not acknowledge the difference in ethnicity, religion or any other expression of diversity, but to treat everyone the same. The important principle here is to recognise and acknowledge difference and to think through the implications of this. In the case of diversity, this means valuing difference and recognising and responding to that difference in a way which meets the needs of individuals appropriately. In the case of workplace culture, this means recognising that there will be a definite culture: that it will be one that is valuing of the adults who are supported; or it may not be valuing of them; or it could even be a mixture of the two. It is totally appropriate that workers support each other and enjoy their work; what is not appropriate is when this is to the detriment of others.

Going back to the example of the Nursing Home used at the beginning of the book, the culture did not value the older people who lived at the home, but was one where they were regarded as a commodity almost, rather than real people with emotional needs as well as care needs. The quicker and more efficiently they could be supported, the better. If a new worker joins a workplace with such a culture, then they learn that speed is important and will quickly pick up on the negative attitude towards the older people, even though it may or may not be directly expressed. To stand out against a prevailing workplace culture is very difficult, especially for new or inexperienced workers. A new worker in that situation might choose to work in a different way from the others, but to challenge the cultural 'norms' is far harder especially as this is to risk rejection. It is however, important that these norms are challenged. The adage, 'if you are not part of the solution, you are part of the problem' might sound harsh, but it is accurate.

Difficult as it is, if your workplace culture is one where the adults you support are not valued and supported appropriately, then it is part of your responsibility to address this. This can be a very daunting task for a worker, especially a new one. Issues such as these should be addressed through staff training and management taking responsibility, but individual workers also have responsibility. Staff in such a situation can feel overwhelmed and maybe even tempted to leave a job rather than address these issues. This would have the effect of reinforcing the cultural values as they are not challenged and if only people that fit in with such a culture work there, there is almost no chance of change.

Family culture

I have written about family carers elsewhere in this book (Chapter 4), and this section should be considered alongside that to give a balanced view. Many adults who receive services continue to live within family units and are therefore to be seen within the context of the individual family culture. Thompson (2006), talking of the practice of social workers, states that they:

> need to adopt a critical stance towards the family, as the traditional social policy eulogy of the family conceals a large number of patriarchal assumptions which fuel the sexism which oppresses women by chaining them to the domestic sphere of caring and nurturing. (p. 59)

Family cultures replicate the assumptions of society which include, as Thompson states, assumptions about gender roles. It can also include assumptions about the value of an individual, which can be based on ageist, sexist, homophobic or disablist assumptions. A person can be viewed as a 'burden' as they require support and may not be able to contribute to the family practically as perhaps they once did. They might be a disabled person and be 'cared for' in such a manner that they are prevented from living in any kind of independent way. They may be a gay or lesbian disabled person who their family controls in terms of opportunities to develop personal relationships because of the homophobia within the family. They may be a disabled adult who is denied any kind of sexual relationship because their family believes that disabled people should not have sexual relationships. A family culture can be the most powerful of all as it is very difficult for an individual to go against what the family believe. Part of safeguarding adults may be to support an adult in challenging some of the values and control imposed on them by their own family. Families that tightly control an adult's life may do so out of what they believe to be the best of motives. However, the outcome for the adult is that they are not permitted to live as independently as they could. The biggest risk to them not achieving the life they would like is not their impairment, illness or age, but the family culture in which they live.

Structural level – S

As I have stated, the personal level is embedded in the cultural level and this in turn is embedded in the structural level. Thompson (1998) states:

> The S level comprises the macro-level influences and constraints of the various social, political and economic aspects of the contemporary social order. (p. 16)

This is the level which seems beyond the scope of individuals to change as it is concerned with powerful and deep-seated influences. In our society in Britain this includes capitalism, patriarchy and the way the state and organisations categorise and treat groups of individuals. The fact that it is still predominantly white men who are in positions where decisions about resources are made is one example of how both racism and sexism can be perpetuated. This does not mean that white men are necessarily deliberately acting in an oppressive way, although this might be the case with some. It means that they are predominantly the group in society with the power to make decisions and these decisions are influenced by their own perspective. It is through societal processes that discrimination can be and is often dispensed. These societal processes in turn are kept in motion by whichever group is the most powerful in society.

The fact that market forces are very much to the fore in community care with the rapid growth of independent and private sector services provision, means that profit margins have become a real factor. This is capitalism at work. One group of society, which in this case is both the adults being supported and those who support them, is the means of another group of society making a profit from them. While this may mean, in theory at least, that there is more choice of service providers, it also means that the support of adults will be only one of the considerations of these providers. There are some excellent service providers, who support and work with adults in an appropriate way, but even they are business people and in our capitalist society, many, although not all, will try to minimise their investment and maximise their profit. One way of doing this is by paying low wages to employees. Low wages often mean inexperienced staff, and while it is good that people are given opportunities to gain experience, a balance has to be found in any team so that some people are more mature in their practice and are able to provide good role models to less experienced members of staff. Also, some adults have such complex needs that it might be wholly inappropriate for inexperienced staff to support them and unfair on both the adult being supported and the member of staff who might be out of their depth.

All staff, whether qualified or not, should receive adequate training to do their job well and in such a way that the adults they support are valued and respected.

Training can be quite expensive and when profit margins are so high on the agenda, employers may look at ways of cutting corners. Again, there are some excellent providers who train their staff to a very high standard, but this may not always be the case. If inexperienced staff are recruited and not offered adequate training then a situation and an environment is being created in which adults will not, and probably cannot, be safeguarded.

As already stated, the structural level is the level which seems beyond the scope of individuals to influence. However, changes can be made at the personal level through that to the cultural level, as I have shown in my discussion on the influence individuals have on workplace culture. So too, can changes be made at the structural level through the cultural level. Lots of small changes which lead to a voice being heard can mean a shift in policy which can effect changes at the structural level. One way in which this can happen is through members of staff speaking out about poor or abusive practice. If a member of staff is worried about practices where they work and they are not being listened to or are unable to address concerns with managers then they are now afforded protection in terms of their employment and victimisation by the Public Interest Disclosure Act 1999, if they make a disclosure to a regulatory body such as CSCI (see Chapter 3). In some circumstances, this may be the only way to effect change, but it should not usually be the first method tried. We are living in an ever-changing society, indeed, it has been said that change is the only constant. It is possible to influence how society changes as it changes in response to individuals and groups of individuals. We all have some influence and can be part of the impetus for change. Even if this is only on a very small scale, it is still important as it could mean the difference for an adult in how they are supported and it could be part of a picture of wider change where individuals are supported to enjoy their rights as citizens rather than experience oppressive practice. Prior to any disclosures to external bodies there would normally be attempts to address practice issues directly in the workplace. However, there may occasionally be a circumstance where 'whistle-blowing' is the only possible way to address an issue. What is important is that staff do not give up their own personal ability to effect change because the problem seems too big for them. If everybody fails to address issues because they seem too large then nothing will ever change; in fact, poor practice is likely to become more entrenched and difficult to change. It is the duty of all staff to address poor and abusive practice when they encounter it.

Racism, sexism, heterosexism, ageism and discrimination against disabled people are all displayed and experienced at the personal and cultural levels, but they are embedded in the structural level. What happens in institutions, in terms of their policies and how they exert power and influence is a part of what happens at the structural level. The term 'institutional racism', has become familiar to us as it was used when referring to the actions of the police towards young black men. The concept of a 'glass ceiling', a metaphor indicating that women can only advance so far in their career or business life and then encounter an invisible barrier which stops them progressing any further is a reference to institutional sexism. These forms of discrimination are perpetuated in our patriarchal society by those in power with a vested interest in keeping things as they are. This is not to say that those in positions of power are necessarily deliberately trying to oppress other sections of society, but they are caught up in the process by which this happens and become a part of how it is continued. They may be totally unaware of how they exert power in a manner which discriminates against some members of society as they may have little insight into the way they are in turn influenced by their culture and how this influences their actions. This may mean that they discriminate by not actually including rather than actively excluding some sections of society, but the impact on those sections is the same regardless of how they were excluded. Again, although the power structures seem way beyond the influence of individuals, change can be brought about by individuals challenging systems and processes to ensure equality issues are addressed. As it can be a matter of a lack of awareness by those in powerful positions, without someone pointing out to them the implications of their policies or practices, nothing will ever change. Understanding how people are discriminated against at the different levels will enable you to view discrimination as a more complex process than just individuals exerting their power. Building on that understanding, it will hopefully encourage you to challenge appropriately as you will understand that as a worker you have the opportunity to be part of bringing about change. You are not just a lone voice, but are part of society and as such have the opportunity to influence how it changes for the better.

A case study might help to illustrate these different forms of discrimination.

Case study

Lorna is a thirty year old black woman with a physical impairment. She lives in her own house and has employed a personal assistant to support her in her personal needs. Prior to Lorna living in her own house, she lived in a large residential home, which was registered for older people. She didn't really like living there as there was no one her own age to talk to and she found the regime of the home difficult to cope with. One thing she didn't like was that everyone had to go to bed before 10 o'clock when the night staff came on duty. Lorna had lived in the residential home for six years because there weren't any vacancies in a residential home for younger people which could meet her needs. Lorna used to like to talk to some of the staff at the home, but she had overheard some of them talking about her and saying that it was a 'shame' that she was 'like that' and that they didn't like the way she ate at mealtimes as Lorna finds it difficult to co-ordinate the use of cutlery and sometimes makes a bit of a mess when she eats. Lorna also struggles to eat the food as it is not what she is used to. She had to eat the food which was prepared for her and although the cook sometimes made the effort to prepare food which was more culturally appropriate for Lorna, it was never cooked very well as the cook did not really know how to cook West Indian food. Lorna is now able to direct her personal assistant in how she likes to be supported and this new experience has made her realise how oppressive her experience in the residential home was. Lorna now cooks her own food, with any support she needs being provided by her personal assistant. She also goes to bed when she likes and generally lives her life as she wants to, not in a way which suits the routines and culture of a residential home.

In the case study, we can see discrimination operating at each of the levels. The personal opinions and comments of the members of staff which Lorna hears is experienced at the personal level. The opinions of the staff members are the result of their own values of who is a valuable person in society. Lorna doesn't seem to fit in with these as she is physically impaired, and this is expressed by the staff members as being 'a shame'. Their expression of distaste at the way she eats shows a lack of sensitivity to her individual needs and the assumption that the way they eat is better betrays a real belief in their own 'superiority' to her. Lorna is discriminated against on the cultural level, as part of the culture of the residential home is that everyone has to be in bed by 10 o'clock. This is a convenience for the staff and has nothing to do with the needs of the people who live in the home. Lorna has already been discriminated against on the structural level by being placed in a residential home for older people. This has happened because there was not a suitable placement in a residential unit for younger people and so local policy and commissioning has failed to take account of her and so discriminated against her. This would of course be against the registration of the home and shouldn't happen.

The reason that such inappropriate placements do occur is that there are not sufficient resources to meet the needs of some people. This is where Lorna experiences structural discrimination. Her misplacement is the result of policy decisions issued by mainly white men who have not experienced what it is like to be in receipt of the implications of their policy outcomes. Lorna's experience of the food not being culturally appropriate is a result of discrimination at the cultural and structural level. At the cultural level, it is assumed that Lorna will eat food which originates from a culture other than her own. This is the approach which treats all people the same and pays no heed to difference. Lorna's cultural needs are not being met and as a result she is being discriminated against. The fact that the cook is unable to cook culturally appropriate food is a result of discrimination at the structural level. Issues such as the ability to cook or willingness to learn to cook culturally appropriate food should have been a recruitment and certainly a training issue. The fact that this issue has not been addressed is either the result of poor policy, or poor application of policy, resulting in bad practice. The intention may not have been to discriminate against anyone, but the end result is that Lorna experiences discrimination. People experience discrimination not only as a result of negative attitudes, but also as a result of ill informed practice.

Values

I have touched on the importance of values earlier in the book. Hofstede (1997) states:

> Values are among the first things children learn – not consciously, but implicitly. Development psychologists believe that by the age of ten, most children have their basic value system in place, and after that age, changes are difficult to make. Because they are acquired so early in our lives, many values remain unconscious to those who hold them. Therefore they cannot be discussed, nor can they be directly observed by outsiders. They can only be inferred from the way people act under various circumstances. (p. 8)

The values we hold inform the way we behave, so it is important to give some consideration to them here. The Collins English Dictionary defines values as 'the moral principles and beliefs or accepted standards of a person or social group'. It can be difficult to identify our beliefs as they may not have the status of 'beliefs' in our mind. If we hold religious beliefs they are somewhat easier to identify as they may be taught in such a way that they are identified as 'beliefs'.

Religious beliefs

I am going to discuss religious beliefs, not because these are the only kinds of beliefs which influence people, but because they provide a useful case example of how personal beliefs shape us and our thinking and ultimately our practice. People from different faith communities are probably aware that they may hold 'beliefs' which are a result of their religion and they are not generally shared by people from outside the faith community. An example would be a belief in an afterlife or a particular account of the formulation of the world. These kinds of religious beliefs are important as they can profoundly influence the way people behave. The current debate in the Church of England about gay rights highlights very powerfully how strongly held religious beliefs are. Moss (2005), in his helpful book on religion and spirituality comments:

> One issue which continues to cause consternation is the way in which the major religions by and large continue to deny the validity of same-sex relationships, and actively ostracise gay and lesbian people from their congregations . . . The holy books are used to justify this position, and it is an issue which is often characterised by a crusading vehemence. Nevertheless, there are many examples of gay Christian clergy continuing to exercise their leadership role, but the comfort zone for them is very slender, and many gay people involved in faith communities are still afraid to 'come out' for fear of reprisals and rejection. (p. 21)

If a person holds a religious belief which means that they believe that a group of people are living 'immoral' lives, then the holder of such beliefs has to give serious consideration to how that affects the way they practice and behave with people. Such views can lead to the conclusion that such 'deviancy' is in need of treatment and is either an illness or a vice. If a person supporting someone who is gay believes that it is part of their moral duty to try and correct what they see as an 'evil' in another, then such a person has a number of options in how they choose to be. Firstly, they might think they can 'leave their beliefs at home'; secondly, have two kinds of thinking, one for work and one for the rest of their life, or thirdly, they will be unable, because of what they believe, to support a person or even just value them in their choice of lifestyle. Think about each of these options and see what you feel about the viability of each. Is the first of these options really an option, as no matter how well people think they can have a set of beliefs and these will not affect their behaviour; is this scenario really possible? Does what you believe influence how you view and therefore treat people? I would say for me that it does, but you have to ask yourself the same question in relation to your own beliefs and the adults you work with. I do think that people can hold a duality of values, but it is not always a comfortable or even an altogether sustainable position. Is the second option again really a viable option? Is it possible to hold two conflicting sets of beliefs according to where you are at a given time? This is a position which requires considerable 'mental gymnastics', but ultimately, how viable is it? The third option is that the person is not supported in an appropriate way as their choices are not respected, which is unacceptable as it places the values of the worker at a higher importance than the person being supported and is basically a denial of their rights. I do not want to be too dogmatic about this as what is important is that you do not dodge the issues for yourself and your own practice, but address them in a way which is honest with yourself.

This is a very difficult area as religious freedom is an important right in this country and people have a right to be a part of and to practice the religion of their upbringing or of their choice. However, anyone who holds views such as believing that gay or lesbian people are deviant or 'sinful' as a result of their sexual identity, needs to think through very carefully how they can possibly support and work with people if they think they are deviant. How can they possibly support adults in their choice of relationships if they believed such relationships are 'wrong'? If you hold such beliefs, take the challenge to think about the difference this makes to your practice and how you can address such issues. If you do not hold such beliefs, but know people who do, do not underestimate the difficulty in which such dilemmas place people. You cannot know the powerful influence of a religious belief if you have not held any, nor can you fully appreciate the personal implications for people if they choose to go against the teaching of religious leaders.

Some writers would agree that it *is* possible to separate personal and professional values. Banks (2006) explores this issue and cites an example, given by Leighton, of a social worker who is a Catholic and holds particular values from his private life, including that abortion is morally wrong and that converting people to Catholicism is desirable, neither of which is in harmony with the professional values of self-determination and being non-judgmental. Banks states that Leighton seems to argue that being a private individual and being a professional are totally different things. Banks questions this:

> But is it? Surely the private individual or person decided to accept the job of social worker with its particular values and duties. If he was the kind of person who was such a strong Catholic that he went around trying to convert neighbours, friends and people in the street and he strongly opposed birth control, then arguably he would not have chosen to become a social worker with this particular agency. (p. 135)

There are many people who do hold different personal values from the professional values they sign up to when they join a particular profession or work for a particular agency. Talking of a social worker when professional and personal values do conflict, Banks states:

> Where they conflict, the social worker as a person has a moral responsibility to decide those that have primacy and to justify this decision. (p. 136)

In the given example, Banks suggests that the social worker might decide he cannot work for the agency as it involves considerable work promoting birth control or he may request to deal only with certain cases. He may feel that he is happier working for a Catholic agency. These possible conflicts of personal and professional values are not confined to social work, of course, and you will be able to identify the areas in your own work where conflict might exist. The idea proposed by Banks that one value system takes primacy over another is an interesting one. For this to happen a worker must be very clear about why there are clashes of values and be sure that they are able to act according to their professional values rather than their personal ones, as this is what they are employed to do. It would certainly be a misuse of power to use opportunities afforded by a professional role to try and convert someone to any religious persuasion. How far it is possible to act in a way that contradicts personal values is debatable. I would say that it is very difficult, but this is an area which you must address for yourself. It is really important that if you have strong personal beliefs, be they religious, political or ideological in origin, you acknowledge any conflict honestly, at least to yourself and preferably to your supervisor, and think through implications for practice. We are thinking about this issue in the context of safeguarding adults, so what is important is that you are able to act in a way that supports individuals' rights to live as independently as possible in the way that they would like to live, and to be free from abuse or harm.

Values as accepted standards

The definition also said that values are 'accepted standards of a person or social group'. We all have values irrespective of any religious beliefs. It is not something you have a choice in; you have them as a result of your upbringing and your culture. You will have absorbed your values without being aware of it. The conversations you heard as a child and young person, the media you watched, listened to and read, the reactions to and actions against certain groups of society and who was the 'butt' of jokes will all have been processed subconsciously and form your value system. This means that in a patriarchal society, you will have taken on board the messages of sexism, that males are superior to females and that the role of a woman is to be subservient to a man. The extent of this will vary according to your own personal history and circumstances and may be more pronounced for some than for others. However, you will have been subject to these messages to some extent whether you are male or female. If you are female, you will have been given the message that your role in life would be to take care of the needs of a man. This is evident all around in homes as well as in work environments where the female workers will 'fuss over' a male manager or colleague purely because he is a man. The man will likewise have been subject to the message that the role of the woman is to meet his needs while he gets on with the more important things in life. Both men and women may be horrified if it is pointed out that they are acting as they do because they hold sexist beliefs and values, as they may honestly believe that they do not. This is important because it tells us something about the nature of values. It tells us that we may realise we hold them, as can be the case with values derived from religious dogma.

Some values, however, we do not consciously realise we have and may even strongly refute that we have. Whether or not these values are at a conscious level or not does not change the fact that they do influence our behaviour. You do not have a choice in the influences that have shaped your thinking, although you do have a choice in whether or not you challenge them and think why you behave as you do and as a result change the way you behave. Without this reflection and resulting change of behaviour, your behaviour will be influenced as in the example of the women in a workplace 'fussing' over the men or even more so if there is only one man; they cannot help themselves, they have been programmed to think this is how women should behave towards men. This seems trivial if it is just a matter of making cups of tea for the men in the workplace, but the reasons behind it are not trivial.

If it is true that we cannot help but act in a way that is in accordance with our values, then this has profound implications for us and more especially for the adults we work with. There are different theories as to the process whereby this happens, but what is important is that we are aware that it does happen. Think of a group of people in society that you have a negative attitude towards. How did you form this attitude? You may think it is through personal experience but the reality is more likely to be that you have had a negative experience with a member of that particular group which just reinforced what you thought before that experience. There will always be some people who can reinforce a negative view, whereas there will be many other representatives of a particular group who do not conform to the negative perception. It is the experiences that reinforce what you believed in the first place that resonate with you rather than any experience you have that contradicts that view. If you have a contrary experience, it is easy to take the attitude 'well, they can't all be bad'. This is not a breakthrough in thinking but again reinforces the negative value as it is 'the exception which proves the rule'.

The values that we hold are so strong that no matter what experiences we have, they can just serve to reinforce them. The implication of this is that as we work with representatives of groups that are not valued by society, then part of the deep-seated values that we hold will just ensure that these people continue to experience discrimination through us. This is what will happen, even if we think we are working in a positive way unless we consciously examine our values and think through the impact of them on how we act. It is possible to challenge the values we hold and so change the way we act but this is an ongoing process. We can realise that we have values that are based on racist, sexist, homophobic or disablist attitudes and can challenge how we think about other people. It is important that we do this but there is not a 'quick fix' solution. As our values inform the way we act, but the process is often an unconscious one, this means that we have to make the unconscious 'conscious'. By this I mean that we have to think about what we believe and why and how this influences the way in which we regard and act towards other people. It is very difficult for those who regard themselves as positive in their attitude towards the adults they work with to identify areas where they are acting in a way that is oppressive. It is difficult because people underestimate the deep and unconscious level at which these values operate and think that they can address the issues in a relatively superficial way.

A lesson from history

An important lesson can be learnt from history on the influence of values and beliefs on the lives of people. Individuals with a learning or physical disability were largely integrated into society and lived with their families until the Victorian times. A number of factors totally changed the experience of disabled people and they all originated with the values and beliefs of society. With the industrialisation of society, disabled people began to be regarded as being of less worth than others because they were unable to keep up with the pace of work required in the new factories. The eugenics movement was a powerful force in Victorian times and contributed to the creation of colonies for disabled people. They were taken away from their families and forced to live a segregated life in institutions which were no more than a tool of the eugenics movement to control those regarded as defective. Part of this control was to stop them having children as there was a great fear of the population being 'infected' and so the racial purity compromised. In the United States this fear led to a programme of sterilisation and of course in Nazi Germany many disabled people were killed in the gas chambers or shot to stop them compromising the purity of the race. The response in Britain was not to sterilise people on a large scale, but to make them live in colonies where they were not permitted to mix with people of the opposite gender.

This extreme form of social control was the direct result of the values of a society which not only didn't value disabled people, but saw them as a threat to future generations. This example seems remote, but its legacy is still with us to this day. There are many people alive today who lived in such institutions, although these later became hospitals. There are still some in existence even though most have closed and people have gone to live in community-based settings. It would be unacceptable now for such extreme forms of social control to exist, but it is still possible for disabled people to have the same experience but expressed and manifested in a much more subtle way. The nature of this more subtle form of social control is that it is harder to detect, as one thing can masquerade as something else. It is possible for someone to think they are acting in the best interests of an individual, for example in encouraging them to make a particular decision, when in reality the person is having their rights denied. If somebody with a learning or physical disability is encouraged to have a sterilisation operation and the reasons given are that they would be unable to look after any children that they might have, then the question to be asked is whether this is really the case, or whether the person encouraging the decision thinks that disabled people should not have children. Again, this is a very complex area and there might be cases where this *is* an appropriate course of action and one that the adult has thought through themselves and is happy with. The question that I think has to be asked though, is whether this is in the interest of the disabled person and any potential children or whether it is just another form of social control where someone is having their rights denied, but in a socially much more acceptable way.

The eugenics movement seems totally alien today and abhorrent, but it was not just the view of a few extremists who were very influential. McClimens (2005) comments:

> Readers will probably recoil from such a world view but it had many adherents in public life in the early decades of the twentieth century. Eugenics was not some esoteric cult movement. It attracted interest and approval from many sections of society. (p. 39)

The point of this observation is that people at the beginning of the twentieth century were as we are today, in that they were informed by attitudes and the values that were current at that time. They will not have regarded themselves as discriminatory (had this even been a point of discussion at the time) but as enlightened and thoughtful people. We can see all too clearly the deficiency in their value systems as we are looking from a different time where societal values have changed. It is a lesson from the past that terrible actions can be carried out by educated and thoughtful people thinking they are acting in an appropriate way. Our job is not to be complacent, as we live in more enlightened times, but to think about our own values and those of the society in which we live and to determine the implications of these for the adults we support.

Points to ponder

This may have been quite a challenging chapter for you to read in terms of thinking through your own value system. Below are listed some questions which might help you reflect further on the issues raised:

➤ Consider what has influenced the way you think, for example what you learnt from your childhood or any political or religious beliefs you might hold.
➤ Do your own personal values clash in any way with the values of your agency or with your professional values? If so, how can you reconcile the two? How will you ensure you act in accordance with professional and agency values?
➤ Do you hold any values or beliefs which make some situations you work with difficult for you?

Conclusion

I have covered a lot of material in this book and I hope that it has been thought-provoking. I have looked at safeguarding adults and the importance of your role in that process. I have shown that safeguarding adults is not only a matter of what used to be called 'adult protection', but is much wider than that. Safeguarding adults concerns every aspect of how we work with and support them in ensuring that they live their lives as independently and safely as possible. I have looked at the role that discrimination plays in the lives of those that we work with and how this operates through different levels.

The thought I want to leave you with is that you have a really important contribution to make to the lives of the people you support and the opportunity to be part of the changing nature of society. What you do will either serve to reinforce discrimination or make you part of a challenge to, and ultimately a change in, society where adults are valued and afforded the dignity they deserve.

Part Four: Guide to Further Learning

This book has served as an introduction to the subject of safeguarding adults. I want to recommend to you some books and websites which I have found particularly useful. However, there are many other books and publications as well as websites which are really helpful and the fact that they are not included here is not a valuation of their worth. I have tried to be selective and to start you on your journey of reflection on your own role in safeguarding the adults you work with. Most of the books recommended would be of use to any professional working with adults, while some are written specifically for social workers in relation to their role as assessors or in using the law. These books would be helpful to you if you are interested in finding out more about these areas, regardless of your professional background or current role. The inclusion of the books, journals and websites here does not mean that I necessarily agree with everything contained in them, but that I consider them to be informative and thought-provoking.

Abuse

Adult abuse is explored in Pritchard (2001). It has useful chapters written by different contributors and covers material not considered in this book, including a helpful chapter on how to interview. The book was written prior to publication of the Department of Health's *Safeguarding Adults* so does not include a discussion on that.

The *Journal of Adult Protection* provides up-to-date articles on the subject of adult abuse. The articles are helpful to practitioners as they are written in accessible language.

There are now a number of new books about 'vulnerable adults' and I would suggest Brown's book (2006) as it provides an exploration of issues in relation to all vulnerable adults.

Older People

Publications addressing practice issues in relation to older people that I would suggest reading are: Thompson, S. (2006), Hugh and Baldwin (2006) and Kitwood (1997). Thompson addresses ageism and the reader is encouraged to explore whether their own practice reinforces or challenges this. Hugh and Baldwin's book considers ethical issues in relation to supporting those with dementia and suggests practical solutions. Kitwood also explores matters raised by working with people with dementia. The book explores the concept of 'personhood' and encourages support to be offered to people with dementia in the context of relationships – a thought-provoking book.

I would suggest Pritchard (2006) for those working with older people, as the book helpfully explores practice in Canada and Britain, giving an overview of practice issues and developments in both countries. It also looks at research, theory, policy and legislation.

Issues in relation to older people, including elder abuse, are contained on the website http://www.ageconcern.org.uk

People with a learning disability

Issues in relation to learning disabled adults are examined in McClimens (2005). This comprehensive book covers a large variety of topics in relation to individuals with a learning disability and I would recommend it if this is the group of people you work with. Another thoughtful book if you work with people with learning disabilities is Thomas and Woods (2003), which emphasises empowerment and inclusion, values and ethics, advocacy and joint working.

http://mencap.org.uk is the website address of this National charity and the site gives links to information and campaigns in relation to learning disabled people.

Williams (1995) details the types of crimes, abuse and victimisation that are experienced by learning disabled adults and offers advice in relation to crime prevention for this group of people and what to do if the crime has already taken place.

The Ann Craft Trust also provides helpful information in relation to adult protection and adults with a learning disability. The website address is http://www.nottingham.ac.uk/sociology/act

People with a physical impairment

http://www.direct.gov.uk/DisabledPeople is a government website which provides information on legislation, policies and services.

http://www.Scope.org.uk is the website for the charity concerned with people with cerebral palsy but it also has information in relation to other physical impairments. There is a really useful practice guide which you can download from this website entitled *The Good Practice Guide for Support Workers and Personal Assistants working with Disabled People with Communication Impairments*.

People with mental health needs

The Mind website address is http://www.mind.org.uk and it provides informative articles on links between mental health and childhood abuse, as well as the 'vulnerability' to abuse of people with a learning disability and mental health needs.

http://www.mentalhealthfoundation/index.asp is another website address for information in relation to learning disabled adults who experience mental health issues.

For those who want a detailed knowledge of legislation and procedures in relation to mental health needs, I would recommend Brown (2006) which is actually written for qualified social workers working within this area of law. It also contains useful sections on mental capacity and the Care Programme Approach.

The Joseph Rowntree Foundation has a website which contains policy issues and research in relation to adult abuse as well as other issues.

The Department of Health website http://www.doh.gov.uk is extremely helpful as it will tell you the latest developments in safeguarding adults and you can download both *No Secrets* and *Safeguarding Adults* from this website.

Law

Community Care law is thoroughly examined in Mandelstam (2005). This is a large book, but it is full of comprehensive explanations and case examples and is an indispensable reference resource. Brayne and Carr (2005) have also written a comprehensive book on social work law. This book informs and explores the role of human rights and professional ethics. There is an interesting discussion on the conflict between the social worker's role in relation to society and the service user.

The law in Scotland is examined in Baillie *et al*. (2003) as the law in relation to vulnerable adults differs from England and Wales. While the previous two books referred to do cover the law in Scotland to an extent, if you practice in Scotland, this will be a helpful book for you as Scottish law is its main concern.

Discrimination

The subjects of power and discrimination are dealt with in Thompson (2006) and the PCS analysis is fully explained in this book. A thought-provoking discussion of oppression in relation to disability is provided by Oliver (1996).

Thompson (1998) looks at issues of power and discrimination in the human services. This book builds on the PCS analysis as outlined in Thompson in his *Anti-Discriminatory Practice*, which is now in its fourth edition (2006).

Values and beliefs

Banks (2006) is a useful book on ethics and values and although it is written for social workers, has a wider application. Moss (2006) is a very readable and thought-provoking book on values and as you read it you are encouraged to reflect on your own values and how these influence you and your work.

The difficult topic of religion and spirituality is the subject of Moss (2005). I found this book to be really useful and thought-provoking. I would recommend it to anyone who would like to explore issues of belief and practice further. This is one of the very few books which address these important matters.

Family carers

For matters pertaining to family carers I recommend the website http://www.carersuk.org. The government has produced a website, http://carers.gov.uk which provides details of services and policies.

Service user participation

http://www.scie-socialcareonline.org.uk is the website of the Commission of Social Care Inspection and there are a number of useful documents which you can download, including one on developing effective service user and carer participation (2006) as well as a paper on whether service user participation has made any difference to social care services (2004).

http://www.shapingourlives.org.uk is the website of an organisation run by service users so provides a really good insight into issues as seen by the recipients of services.

Person centred planning and assessment

Person centred planning is explored in Cambridge and Carnaby (eds) (2006) and this contains the principles of PCP as well as case studies and pointers for practice. Although it is written to be applicable for learning disabled adults, the principles are transferable to other groups.

Parker and Bradley (2005) address issues in relation to social work assessment and review. It is specifically written for social work students on the degree in social work, but is helpful for qualified practitioners wanting to refresh their knowledge or other professionals wanting to understand the principles of assessment.

Service improvement

The *Journal of Integrated Care, Practical Evidence for Service Improvement*, published by Pavilion is an excellent source of articles relating to providing a service which values adults.

http://www.scie.org.uk is the website of the Social Care Institute for Excellence which seeks to develop and promote knowledge about good practice in social care.

http://www.nice.org.uk is the website for the National Institute for Clinical Excellence which was set up to make recommendations in relation to treatments and care provided by the NHS.

References

Association of Directors of Social Services (2005) *Safeguarding Adults: A National Framework of Standards for Good Practice and Outcomes in Adult Protection Work*, London: ADSS.

Baillie, D., Cameron, K., Cull, L., Roche, J. and West, J. (eds) (2003) *Social Work and the Law in Scotland*, Palgrave Macmillan.

Banks, S. (2006) *Ethics and Values in Social Work*, 3rd edn, Palgrave Macmillan.

Bichard Inquiry (2005) http://www.bichardinquiry.org.uk

Brayne, H. and Carr, H. (2005) *Law for Social Workers*, 9th edn, Oxford University Press.

British Association of Social Workers (BASW) (1975) *The Code of Ethics for Social Work*, Birmingham, BASW.

Brown, K. (ed.) (2006) *Vulnerable Adults and Community Care: A Reader*, Learning Matters Ltd.

Buckner, L. and Yeandle, S. (2006) *What Carers Need*, http://www.carersuk.org

Cambridge, P. and Carnaby, S. (ed.) 2005) *Person Centred Planning and Care Management with People with Learning Disabilities*, Jessica Kingsley Publishers.

Care Standards Act 2000, London, HMSO.

Carers and Disabled Children Act 2000, London, HMSO.

Carers (Equal Opportunities) Act 2004, London, HMSO.

Children Act 1989, London, HMSO.

Commission for Social Care Inspection (2004) *Position paper 3: Has Service User Participation Made a Difference to Social Care Services?* http://www.scie-socialcareon-line.org.uk

Commission for Social Care Inspection (2006) *Developing Measures for Effective Service User and Carer Participation*, http://www.scie-socialcareonline.org.uk

Crime and Disorder Act 1998, London, HMSO.

Data Protection Act 1998, London, HMSO.

Department of Health (1997) *Young Carers – Something to Think About. Report of four SSI workshops May-June 1995*, London, HMSO.

Department of Health (1999a) *Caring for Carers*, London, HMSO.

Department of Health (1999b) *National Service Framework for Mental Health*, London, HMSO.

Department of Health (2000) *No Secrets: Guidance on Developing and Implementing Multi-Agency Policies and Procedures to Protect Vulnerable Adults from Abuse*, London, HMSO.

Department of Health (2001) *Valuing People: A New Strategy for Learning Disability for the 21st Century*, London.

Department of Health (2002) *Fair Access to Care Services: Guidance on Eligibility Criteria for Adult Social Care*, London, HMSO.

Department of Health (2004) *The Government's Response to the Recommendations and Conclusions of the Health Select Committee's Inquiry into Elder Abuse*, London, HMSO.

Department of Health (2006) *Our Health, Our Care, Our Say: A New Direction for Community Services*, London, HMSO.

Domestic Violence, Crime and Victim's Act 2004, London, HMSO.

Drug Trafficing Offences Act 1986, London, HMSO.

Duffy, S. (2006) 'The Implications of Individual Budgets', in *Journal of Social Care, Practical Evidence for Service Improvement*, 14, (2).

Duffy, S. and Sanderson, H. (2005) 'Relationships between Care Management and Person Centred Planning' in Cambridge, P. and Carnaby, S. (eds) *Person Centred Planning and Care Management with People with Learning Disabilities*, Jessica Kingsley.

Hofstede, G. (1997) *Cultures and Organisation, Software of the Mind*, McGraw-Hill.

Hugh, J. and Baldwin, C. (2006) *Ethical Issues in Dementia Care: Making Difficult Decisions*, Jessica Kingsley.

Human Rights Act 1998, London, HMSO.

Kitwood, T. (1997) *Dementia Reconsidered: The Person Comes First*, Open University Press.

Kurrle, S. (2001) 'The Role of the Medical Practitioner. A View from Australia' in Pritchard, J. (ed.) (2001), *Good Practice with Vulnerable Adults*, Jessica Kingsley.

Lamb, L. (2000) *Would 'No Secrets' have saved Beverley?* www.sense.org.uk/publications/allpubs/magazine/tsarticles/2000/nosecrets.htm

Mandelstam, M. (2005) *Community Care Practice and the Law*, Jessica Kingsley.

Local Authority Social Services Act 1970, London, HMSO.

Mansell, J. and Beadle-Brown, J. (2005) 'Person-Centred Planning and Person-Centred Action', in *Person Centred Planning and Care Management with People with Learning Disabilities*, Jessica Kingsley.

Manthorpe, J., Perkins, N., Penhale, B., Pinkley, L. and Kingston, P. (2005) 'Select questions: considering the issues raised by a Parliamentary Select Committee Inquiry into Elder Abuse', *Journal of Adult Protection*, 7, (3) 19–31.

McClimens, A. (2005) 'The Construction of Learning Disability', in Grant, G., Goward, P., Richardson, M. and Ramsharan, P. (eds) *Learning Disability: A Life Cycle Approach to Valuing People*, Open University Press.

Mental Capacity Act, 2005, London, HMSO.

Mental Health Act, 1983, London, HMSO.

Milner, J. and O'Byrne, P. (2002) *Assessment in Social Work*, 2nd edn, Palgrave.

Moss, B. (2005) *Religion and Spirituality*, Lyme Regis, Russell House Publishing.

Moss, B. (2006) *Values*, Lyme Regis, Russell House Publishing.

National Assistance Act 1948, London, HMSO.

NHS and Community Care Act 1990, London, HMSO.

Oliver, M. (1996) *Understanding Disability, From Theory to Practice*, Macmillan.

Parker, J. and Bradley, G. (2005) *Social Work Practice: Assessment, Planning, Intervention and Review*, Exeter: Learning Matters Ltd.

Pritchard, J. (ed.) (2001), *Good Practice with Vulnerable Adults*, London, Jessica Kingsley.

Pritchard, J. (ed.) (2006) *Elder Abuse Work. Best Practice in Britain and Canada*, London, Jessica Kingsley.

Public Interest Disclosure Act 1998, London, HMSO.

Sanderson, H., Thompson, J. and Kilbane, J. (2006) 'The Emergence of Person-Centred Planning as Evidence-Based Practice', in *Journal of Integrated Care, Practical Evidence for Service Improvement*, 14, (2), Pavilion.

Sexual Offences Act 2003, London, HMSO.

Taylor, K. and Dodd, K. (2003) 'Knowledge and Attitudes of Staff towards Adult Protection', in *Journal of Adult Protection* 5, (4) 26–32, Pavilion.

Thomas, D. and Woods, H. (2003) *Working with People with Learning Disabilities*, London, Jessica Kingsley.

Thompson, N. (1998) *Promoting Equality, Challenging Discrimination and Oppression in the Human Services*, Basingstoke, Palgrave Macmillan.

Thompson, N. (2006a), *Anti-Discriminatory Practice*, 4th edn, Basingstoke, Palgrave Macmillan.

Thompson, S. (2006b) *Age Discrimination*, Lyme Regis, Russell House Publishing.

Watson, J. (2006) *Whose Rights are they Anyway? Carers and the Human Rights Act*, www.carersuk.org

Webb, R. and Tossell, D. (1999) Social Issues for Carers, 2nd edn, in *Towards Positive Practice*, Arnold.

Williams, C. (1995) *Crime and Abuse against People with Learning Disabilities*, London, Jessica Kingsley.

Wood, J. and Watson, P. (2000) *Working with Family Carers, A Guide to Good Practice*, Age Concern.

Index

▌▌▌ Theory into Practice

Other books in this series include:

Religion and Spirituality
By Bernard Moss

978-1-903855-57-7   2005

Power and Empowerment
By Neil Thompson

978-1-903855-99-7   2007

Age Discrimination
By Sue Thompson

978-1-903855-59-1   2005

Community Care
By Neil Thompson and Sue Thompson

978-1-903855-58-4   2005

Values
By Bernard Moss

978-1-903855-89-8   2007

Full details can be found at www.russellhouse.co.uk and we are always pleased to send out information to you by post.
Our contact details are at the front of this book.